The
Steps
We
Take

The
Steps
We
Take

A Memoir of
Southern
Reckoning

ELLEN ANN FENTRESS

University Press of Mississippi / Jackson

Willie Morris Books in Memoir and Biography

The University Press of Mississippi is the scholarly publishing agency of the Mississippi Institutions of Higher Learning: Alcorn State University, Delta State University, Jackson State University, Mississippi State University, Mississippi University for Women, Mississippi Valley State University, University of Mississippi, and University of Southern Mississippi.

www.upress.state.ms.us

Designed by Peter D. Halverson

The University Press of Mississippi is a member of the Association of University Presses.

The names and identifying details of some individuals have been changed to respect their privacy.

First printing 2023
∞

Library of Congress Cataloging-in-Publication Data

Names: Fentress, Ellen Ann, author.
Title: The steps we take : a memoir of southern reckoning / Ellen Ann Fentress.
Other titles: Willie Morris books in memoir and biography.
Description: Jackson : University Press of Mississippi, 2023. | Series: Willie Morris books in memoir and biography | Includes bibliographical references.
Identifiers: LCCN 2023012269 (print) | LCCN 2023012270 (ebook) | ISBN 9781496847751 (hardback) | ISBN 9781496847768 (epub) | ISBN 9781496847775 (epub) | ISBN 9781496847782 (pdf) | ISBN 9781496847799 (pdf)
Subjects: LCSH: Fentress, Ellen Ann. | Journalists—Mississippi—Biography. | Teachers—Mississippi—Biography. | Motion picture producers and directors—Mississippi—Biography. | Mississippi—Social life and customs—Anecdotes. | Mississippi—Biography.
Classification: LCC CT275.F468 A3 2023 (print) | LCC CT275.F468 (ebook) | DDC 976.2092 [B]—dc23/eng/20230323
LC record available at https://lccn.loc.gov/2023012269
LC ebook record available at https://lccn.loc.gov/2023012270

British Library Cataloging-in-Publication Data available

To the real Kate and Molly. Always my heart, always my teachers.

Contents

The
Steps
We
Take

Introduction

"WHATSOEVER THY HAND FINDEST TO DO, DO IT WITH THY MIGHT." Like iron syrup spilling out of a bottle, that Ecclesiastes verse puddled inside my waiting skull before age six. The leaders at North Greenwood Baptist Church Sunday School were dogged, and my eager head primed.

I like to help. Why is that? Nurture and nature. There were those Old Testament words tucked into me by the time I could balance on a teeny wooden Sunday school–room chair. Also perhaps I'm a little disposed to pious intentions. I arrived at my Baptist college set to become a social worker, possibly in the overseas-mission field. I scrapped those plans in one day once I heard the mournful resignation of the Intro to Sociology professor's vocal cords. His delivery was my idea of propofol. That fast change of heart and life goal is proof that there's more to good intentions than only the rational outer story. What goes on down deep is the kicker and my focus here.

White southern women get their signature memo about helping from family and from the culture. Doing nice things for free is something the world smiles on in our case. (In contrast to controlling our own bodies, thanks to the Mississippi case *Dobbs v. Jackson Women's Health Organization*, which scuttled *Roe* nationally in 2022.) We cook wild rice and sausage casseroles for traumatized friends, buy jokey birthday cards, and say yes to leading Sunday school, T-ball leagues, and parent associations. Tammy Wynette spoke musically for a lot of us when she sang about standing by her man, whom she hinted was far from flaw-free. A stanza or so of my own cover of that female-helpfulness classic is part of the story here. Women

3

may stand by partners in a similar way around the globe, true, but Tammy's Itawamba County, Mississippi, upbringing is on pitch with her mindset and her anthem. I'm just saying.

Things like roofs, groceries, and a ho-hum expectation of outer security numb as well as comfort. That's been my case. I've spent years tending strictly to the low-hanging good-deeds fruit in my vicinity and carefully turning my gaze from the rest. I've neglected to lift my eyes and standards. Is holding on tightly to what I have and know really the top option? I know better.

Those 9:45 a.m. Sunday-morning teachers of mine were well meaning when they drilled us to listen, sing, and pray. In my thirties, I did a turn as a Sunday school teacher of five-year-olds too. A little appreciation, please. After all, we could be home polishing our nails or chucking church altogether to be first in line at a Sunday lunch spot of choice. In my Greenwood girlhood, my pick was the buffet at the Travel Inn on US 82, which, in my opinion, particularly crushed it when it came to pink roast beef and sweaty little footed glass dishes of house-made vanilla ice cream.

Notice how fast I got to appreciation here. More precisely, I mean a helper's expectation of admiration from observers, not even exclusively from the one who was helped. To help and then to expect appreciation is a classic two-step, a dance move that breaks out through sheer muscle memory. Help can get weaponized into a battering ram. One variation from southern whites is the question about gratitude—call it debt—to ancestors whose two-centuries-old DNA came down to us along with their horrific legacy for us to reckon with. We don't owe great-great-grandparents anything, least of all delusions of loyalty that link to white supremacy. Through history and societies, one generation supposedly hopes the next does better. The true way to address ancestry is for the living to do their part to make things right, or at least move toward it.

Poking around the help-acknowledgement balance inevitably provokes uproar in cases both intimate and public. Sometimes the uproar stays locked in one's stomach knot, perpetually suppressed in silence. "But you ought to be grateful" is a gateway guilt cudgel—predictable level 101 stuff—when inside a family, one member starts to question the gratitude tradeoffs. Let's just say I can spot that coming to bloom when I get a whiff. It's familiar.

The bait and switch is a little sneakier, whether on the global scale of, say, running a colonial empire—somehow that's supposed to be cause for appreciation—or congratulating oneself for handing over old yellowed T-shirts to an underpaid housekeeper or a devastated hurricane survivor. The working component of the bait and switch is mistaking strokes to the ego with showing up with authentic support. The bait and switch is no help at all or, just as likely, actively harmful.

Life requires uproars. Things don't get better short of them. Instigating confrontation and being an ally are both the right steps at the right moment. Thankfully there are white southern women who understand that—I name a few in this book—although the cases are too little, too late. It's not as if southern women throughout history weren't capable of mass action—all those Confederate courthouse monuments were built thanks to the Daughters of the Confederacy rewriting reality into a magnolia-laden lie to revive their defeated men. Causes women did champion reinforced the white supremacist status quo or posed no threat to it. For every activist organization, whether it was the Association of Southern Women for the Prevention of Lynching or Wednesdays in Mississippi, there were antiequality groups: the women's division of the Citizens' Council and Women for Constitutional Government.

At age twenty-two I was drawn to journalism, thrilled with the admission ticket into collective life that came with a cub reporter's job. Let's face it, though. It's not as if it took much to qualify as a wider world than mine at Mississippi College and in my Delta hometown at the moment I strode out with my spiral notebook and first story assignment. I latched onto the old saying about journalism's aim being to comfort the afflicted and afflict the comfortable. I thought I could help. Journalism stretched me more than I've stretched it, though. All the encounters challenged my eyes and insides. I buy that the unexamined inner life is less than a life at all.

I know I can mine the universe in my life's grain of sand. But then again, I am only one grain of sand on the beach. There are approximately a bazillion other grains, too, bumping up close to my gritty self, all with much to say and to teach, even if I wasn't perceptive enough to put words to that truth when I was young.

In these pages, I write about taking steps to help in my time and place or at least to try. Yet equally so, sometimes the point in a story is that a choice was made not to give help, maybe on my part or on the culture's, perhaps clearly stated out loud or not. There are stories of help received or denied, misfires, and washouts. Often the one who needed help the most was me.

Humans are herd animals, of course. That means looking at myself through the lens of my assorted outreaches to others is a pretty primary approach. Since southern culture expects women to be available to support others and doubles down by praising women when they do, this line of sight is a particularly good window into a woman's life. Like big-stakes lint, a life's associated details and truths inevitably show up through the good-deeds glass simultaneously.

Also handy is the advice of Carl Jung in *The Red Book*: "If you go to thinking, take your heart with you. If you go to love, take your head with you. Love is empty without thinking, thinking hollow without love." The double head and heart tests are a crucial application as we chew on humans—by that I mean me—and help. What's given? What's received? What's withheld? Why? Let's step in and consider together. I'd love to help you.

Part 1

On Taking Steps . . . or Not

Chapter 1

Volunteering (1)

WOMEN DO A LOT FOR FREE, NO MATTER THE ERA, NO MATTER the location. As a volunteer, I've always brought along more than altruism. My jobs have been indicators of seasons in my life and the place around me. The efforts were telltales of their times: Jennifer Aniston haircuts of good intentions. Through the lens of how I volunteered, you could see the shape of what else was at work within and surrounding me.

My rookie task for an adult cause was when, as an eleventh grader in 1973, I signed up to knock on doors for March of Dimes' annual drive one Sunday afternoon in February. I was already the dateless high school–club type available to do this kind of volunteer job, but I was particularly up for this because (1) I'd superabsorbed a decade of hometown March of Dimes telethons on WABG-TV and (2) peeping inside strangers' homes intrigued me, considering the short-leashed tininess of my existence. Getting a rise out of knocking on strange doors when you're sixteen sounds pretty minuscule, but then again my options were pretty minuscule. No one would disagree either. I did not have a lot going on.

To the rest of my squad inside my friend Tanya's family Buick LeSabre, our canvassing that afternoon represented one more check mark, the kind of thing that Cathy Club high school girls do. While we all earnestly ticked off the boxes when it came to pep squad, church choir, and yearbook staff, my friends' lives stretched further than mine. They had at least minimal dating lives and the kind of flirtations that eluded me, a clear point of shame in Mississippi Delta high school culture.

In 1973, pretty much the entire population of US white high school girls could moonily sing all the words to Carole King's "So Far Away." We broke down further into two types. The first group—my friends fit here—had a particular missing person to croon about. Maybe a someone who'd gone to college, maybe someone from last summer's Methodist camp. Then there was the second category: my own. I sang as wistfully and woefully as anyone, although I was aware I had no one to miss. Yet something ineffable was far away from me. I guess I sang in honor of the cloudy but stubborn sense that there was an empty spot inside me. I missed whatever it was that would fill the vacuum, although I couldn't have articulated that truth. I didn't know consciously what I didn't know. All I knew to do was push the Carole King *Tapestry* tape into the car eight-track and self-serenade. A dog yowls because it can.

One consequence of having too much time on my hands and space in my insides was overthinking any possible spark of promise that did come my way. That Sunday, the flicker was the prospect of knocking on strangers' doors. It went without saying, even in the mid-1970s, that we'd be sent to a white segregated neighborhood only, so there was a slim chance that people inside the houses would have lives much different from people I knew. Yet I could imagine. I could hope. What did I crave? I couldn't say. All I knew was that the chance to knock on doors held a brighter glow than not knocking.

What's more, March of Dimes wasn't just any generic charity. It had TV legs. There was a Marshall McLuhan–style, the-media-is-the-message lure to the March of Dimes built by the annual winter telethon. I'm not sure if March of Dimes was actually Greenwood's biggest civic cause or if it was just the one I was able to see, thanks to the broadcast. Every February, I'd stretch out on the carpet in front of our Admiral console in the den. As Friday night unfolded, the two announcers switched off between urging phone-in pledges and introducing the tap dance acts and gospel quartets. Canned national March of Dimes messages from, say, Elvis Presley or the Everly Brothers, were interspersed. Before the Everlys sang "Bye Bye Love," Don Everly explained, "You know it was the money our parents gave to the March of Dimes that made possible the polio protection we enjoy today—the protection of the Salk vaccine. Well, now it's time for us to think ahead. We teenagers, pretty soon, we'll be having children of our own. We want them to be born with every chance to live happy, normal lives." The telethon was where actual Greenwood people rotated on the screen. I saw people I recognized on the silvery screen, same as the stars, and I wanted to be a part of it somehow.

TV sets up a particular loop in only children, and I was one of them. I watched TV because the adults around me were occupied. Then as I watched programs, the shows reflected that adults engage in interesting events. So I got a double dose of the idea that it's what adults do that matters. That meant the things I did didn't so much. I always suspected playgrounds, classrooms, tap class, and Baptist Sunbeams were holding pens, things for me to do while waiting to become an adult. In early grades, I never grasped peer conversation over our paste jars or got why cooties mattered. Adult endeavors were where the preferred action was anyway, my smarting little ego hoped.

One particular thing lots of adults did in Greenwood, the den TV told me, was pull out the stops for March of Dimes. Every year the station manager Lane Tucker and the weathercaster Calton Crowell vivaciously shot the on-air breeze as viewers called in donations. Local acts lined up at the TV station, a squat celery-green concrete building fronting a cotton field along US 82 West. There'd be a big-energy tap dance rendition of "Happy Talk" by a hair-sprayed eight-year-old and the lip sync of a wispy young man whose mournful eyebrows lifted through the sad-drinker anthem "Make the World Go Away." Seventies or not, you'd never know Leflore County was majority Black since everyone on the show was white. The broadcast lasted through the weekend, so pretty much anyone with a baton or jazz shoes got airtime, should that whiteness box be checked.

Periodically the studio camera panned to the telephone bank where volunteers from the telephone company scribbled down pledges to the sound of ringing landlines. A few times hourly, Lane

Tucker and Calton Crowell would read out more donors, sometimes names of adults I recognized from our Baptist church: "Mrs. Bernice McMann has pledged ten dollars and challenges all other mothers of healthy children to do the same." I knew the McManns' daughter. We sat at the same table in study hall sometimes, and she did look healthy. My parents, however, never seemed to buy into the stakes of the broadcast as I did; certainly they never called in a double-dare pledge like Mrs. McMann's. In fact, they would go about their Friday night without paying much attention to the telethon at all while I stayed glued to the screen. They'd have dinner, clean up afterward, and maybe putter and flip through mail and the afternoon *Greenwood Commonwealth*.

The most mesmerizing parts of the show were the hair-sprayed little girls in wheelchairs and wet-combed little boys with crutches brought in as March of Dimes beneficiaries. My focus centered on the fact that they were on TV, however. I empathized with the little girls in poufy party dresses and their inability to walk, yet I was also jealous of their starring role. Phone pledge after phone pledge, tap dance after tap dance, everyone on the telethon seemed to matter. By 1973, the Greenwood telethon was an event of the past. Even so, the old memory of March of Dimes' proximity to star power stayed in my head, investing it with a lingering layer of importance.

On that Sunday afternoon, we picked up our official collection gear at the chamber of commerce building. My friend Tanya drove us four to our assigned street in her family's metallic fawn LeSabre, the same hue as frosted drugstore lipstick. We all had cardboard buckets, and I had a vague private hope that something of note might happen to me.

"So Far Away" was undoubtedly on the car eight-track because it was on during our car rides every Sunday for three years. Our assigned street stretched through an older, less familiar neighborhood, one school zone away from our part of town. Tanya parked the LeSabre at one end of the line of 1920s bungalows. Every third or fourth house, an old oak presided at the curb, the survivors of what must have been a dense line of trees canopying the street in its prime.

The paint jobs and front yards showed age too. The neighborhood was nearer to downtown than our ranch houses across the Yazoo, the course of the town's post–World War II drift. To ranch house dwellers like us, this neighborhood looked a tad frayed, entirely a plus to me and my hope for something noteworthy to occur.

I'd like to think that all my unnamed longing put me in good historic company. I say that based on a story told by the poet Mary Ruefle in her lecture "*My* Emily Dickinson" published in *Madness, Rack, and Honey*. Prepping for a Dickinson lecture, Ruefle mulled her half-formed sense that the lives of Emily Brontë, Emily Dickinson, and Anne Frank had something in common. Ruefle couldn't put her finger on it, though. On hearing the three names, her friend, a retired teacher, grasped it. "They have no experience of the world," the friend said. Her friend was right, Ruefle realized. "To have no experience of the world—is passion for it. Not passion for experience of the world, but passion for the world." Ruefle reflected, "Deprivation is desire. Isolation is lust."

I was lusting in the Buick, inflamed in a parallel way to that hallowed literary trio. I jumped out of the back seat with my tub.

"Tanya and I'll do this side," I said.

A good sport, Tanya went along with it. "Meet you back here."

"We can do this pretty fast," Katherine said. She and Ann headed to the first house across the street. Katherine didn't intend to draw the job out because her boyfriend, George, was waiting to come over later.

Tanya and I stepped onto the porch of our first house where a dozen or so spider plants in individual mix-and-match plastic cups crowded a table. That many of the same plant, carefully divided and repotted, signaled an older woman, I imagined. A lady in a pink housecoat opened her door. She gauged us through the screen door.

"Hello! We're here for the March of Dimes. Would you like to make a donation?" I asked.

My mouth and Tanya's lifted in the bright, polite, scripted smiles you were supposed to offer older people in public. In my eagerness, I didn't give Tanya a chance to talk. I tried to scrutinize the living room, but the lights were off. A whiff floated through the screen door, sweet as drugstore bath powder and time.

"You girls are mighty smart to be doing this," the woman said, showing a kind smile through the steel mesh. "Let me see." She scuffed away with sighing slipper steps. My blue ballpoint dug into the first line on the cardboard form to record the street number.

The slipper sound returned along with the woman, her loose pink housecoat floating slightly as she moved back into the daylight. She was a half-lit Vermeer figure if Vermeer women zipped into pink loungewear. The screen-door hinges creaked, and her thin-skinned, veined hand dropped two clinking quarters in my tub. I hadn't given the money any thought until now nor had I considered what was a good or cheap donation.

"Thank you so much," I said. "Could I get your name?"

"Edna Jackson." She scanned our faces. "Now who are you girls?" When our names rang no bell, she wished us luck.

I minded the tub, careful that the two quarters didn't fly out. On to the next porch of a Dutch Colonial with a rounded doorway and gray-painted clapboard. The older woman who opened the door smiled at us.

"Good afternoon!" the woman said. Voices on the TV mumbled behind her. I let Tanya talk.

"Ma'am, we're collecting for the March of Dimes. Would you like to make a donation please?" Tanya's sweetly reedy voice uptalked the perky-girl way.

Grown-ups liked Tanya. Her whole face lit up in a big beam when she smiled, her high baby-face cheeks grazing her crinkling eyes. Tanya was a charmer not only to adults but also, I'd noted, to the boys at St. John's Methodist's youth group. Her church was home to the top-tier youth fellowship in town, where they sang Crosby, Stills, Nash & Young along with hymns and, at summer Morning Prayer breakfasts, served hot New Orleans beignets in a blizzard of powdered sugar.

The woman in the doorway said, "Let me see what's in my pocket-book." She went to look.

Across the street, Ann and Katherine had made it to their third front yard, moving through a blob of sun on the winter-dead grass. They climbed the front steps flanked by a pair of stubby, leafless crepe myrtle bushes.

Our Dutch Colonial dweller dropped her two quarters in Tanya's tub.

"Thank you *so* much," we chimed. In quotidian conversations for girls in Mississippi, anything less than over-the-top, performative sunniness comes across as rude. It's a high, frankly exhausting, bar, then and now.

One door after another, it was becoming clear that the grand-mothers who kindly plunked coins in our tubs were similar to my own grandmother: robe loving, conventional, nice, and smelling like Jergen's. What about my hopes that the afternoon would be a portal to something different? A big payoff was not looking good.

The final block on our side of the street was a shady old cemetery. No longer in use, the cemetery featured a flimsy wire fence and a dusty green historic marker that noted forty Confederate soldiers rested under the oaks in its five weedy acres. I looked over the grounds in the moss-dark shade and couldn't help but sigh in identification of an occupant I'd heard about. Athene Oretto rested in the cemetery alongside her parents Otto and Lena Oretto. I had read an old newspaper story that put it this way: "The Orettos were showboat people, who forsook the glamour of the river stage, and settled in Greenwood." Being a showboat person must have been like being in Congress or the NFL; the bona fides turn into bank for a lifetime. The Orettos opened the Rice Hotel in Greenwood, which thrived on their star power. A 1920s Greenwood newspaper piece told the story of their daughter, Athene, born in 1899, stating, "They gave their baby a stage name, perhaps in hope that some day she would be a famous actress. But the day after Christmas, thirty-seven years ago, Baby Athene Oretto died." It continued, "Her little grave is overgrown with brambles, and the tiny headstone so defaced with time and weather, that the inscription is almost obliterated."

Athene's story stuck with me. I felt some sort of tragic identity with the thwarted girl. Despite her show business parents, despite hitching myself to the March of Dimes machinery, our paths had stalled out. Athene was potentially made for a wider world, as I thought I was too. Here among the tombstones was proof that hope only takes some Greenwood girls so far.

I'd had a good Sunday, true. I was tooling around with my girl squad, which was what we aimlessly did every Sunday afternoon anyway. After church and lunch with our own families, we customarily went out riding in one of our parents' defiant, clunky gas guzzlers. We'd loop the north Greenwood streets, pausing at least once at the Humpty Dumpty food mart for Cokes and barbecue Fritos. Back on the streets, we waggled our powdery barbecue-orange fingers through the windows at other cars, honking at the brick houses of people we liked. We mulled whether to wave at approaching Cutlasses or Trans Ams of teens more popular or older than we. Our ego hung in the balance because it was a total slap if they didn't wave back. For me, the ride's top comfort was being snug inside the car with my friends. I went mute around an actual adolescent boy. Chances of any change in my situation weren't promising. If March of Dimes wasn't panning out as a game changer that day, I can't say I wasn't used to frustration anyway.

Despite the jingle of a street's worth of quarters inside the March of Dimes tub, my own life was no wider than it had been before we stepped up to Edna Jackson's starter door. Hitching myself to March of Dimes hadn't changed anything. All of us in the Buick had come to the end of the road, literally.

Then near the cemetery fence and Athene's grave, I realized how one significant door was also quite close to us. The residence wasn't technically on our assigned street, but the side of the house was. The arts and crafts bungalow, with peeling white paint, had been separated into multiple apartments. A dirt-specked window-unit air conditioner jutted out of one of the house's back windows near the plain solid front door of the apartment unit I now targeted. That apartment faced our street.

Here's why the place was of note: On our Sunday rides, we occasionally saw two women outside in the grassless yard. The duo had neon-pink cheeks, sky-high bouffant coal-black hair, and black eyeliner of Magic Marker proportion. Prostitutes, we'd concluded. The notion that these two women matter-of-factly defied our town's prim public parameters far eclipsed any shock about the sex part of the equation. It was their capacity to chuck the expectations of the Greenwood order that intrigued me.

I didn't wait to debate it with the others. I exited the back seat and bolted across the meager yard and up the concrete stairs to their scuffed, windowless door. A little slanted asphalt-shingled ledge hung over the top step. I moved fast, assuming fate would stop me as it typically did. Opportunity knocks, it's said. So did I on the white-painted door in front of me, keeping a death clamp on my March of Dimes tub with the other hand.

The door swung back. Two feet away, one of the high-haired women stared back at me through those eyes looped in sooty circles.

"Hey there," the woman said. Her smile and welcome were friendly. She had the sharp smell of cigarettes. Close up, lines cut more deeply around her mouth than I'd seen when I'd looked at her through the car window on our Sunday rides. The skin crumpled in folds around her eyes as well. Her sprayed, frothy dark hair jutted skyward. She was as mild and unhurried as the conventional grandmothers on the street had been while waiting for me to find my tongue, though. She blinked and paused.

"I'm collecting for the March of Dimes." I flapped the official donation form in my hand to demonstrate my authority.

"Sure, hon," she said. "Let me get something." She disappeared into the shadow of the interior.

I noticed that two men in plaid sports shirts were sitting in the dark living room. They nodded hello to me from their chairs and went back to the TV. Tobacco smoke along with a stale whiff of old fried food floated out to where I stood on the front step. Tanya, Ann, and Katherine took in the exchange through the glass of the Buick with mild gazes. They were patient but ready to go home and retool for 6 p.m. Sunday-night youth group at their churches.

The second woman materialized in the doorway with a calm look and quarter-inch-thick black eyeliner that matched her friend's.

"Hey there," she said. She'd come to size up who'd knocked.

Me. My once jumbo-curled hair was hopeless frizz in the overcast February dankness. I'd worn my favorite ribbed yellow- and red-striped U-neck sweater and bell-bottom Wranglers.

"Hello." I hoped my beaming smile looked friendly. I didn't want to come across as the hungry gawker I was.

Their Sunday-afternoon clothes were pretty much basic Greenwood mom attire—casual, mix-and-match picks of nondescript dark pants and equally nondescript front-buttoning tops. The outfits were what anyone's mother might wear to the grocery store. Their living room was dowdy and run-down, the kind of frayed feminine space that one of my own great-aunts might have.

The first woman returned. "Here you go." Her long maroon fingernails stretched over the threshold, dropping a dollar bill into my tub. This was our biggest donation of the day.

"Would you fill out the form, please?"

"Sure." She reached for the Bic. Her red nails posed no trouble as she printed: SHIRLEY HILBURN.

"Thank you very much." I tried to sound businesslike.

"You're welcome."

Back at the LeSabre, as I yanked the door handle, I felt a rush, possibly a current, circling within that forlorn, empty spot I customarily sensed inside me. Not much had technically happened, of course, in collecting Shirley Hilburn's dollar. Yet I had encountered new territory at the two women's threshold. I'd seen women who took their circumstances and seized the agency that they could. Not everything was possible, but they pushed the outer limits of their givens.

In eighteen months, I'd leave Greenwood for college. I wasn't the only one standing at the doorway of change, though. March of Dimes was going to morph as well. Founded in the Franklin D.

Roosevelt era, the charity educated a previously uninformed country about others who live with polio and arthritis and, later, birth defects. Yet it also framed donating as what "normal" nondisabled people do for those whom they regard as "abnormal." Also, a few years later, the term *prostitute* fell out of use, giving way to the less judgmental job description of *sex worker*. A job isn't any human's full identity, or shouldn't be, anyway.

In Jackson, Mississippi, I have a friend, Janie, who grew up in Greenwood a few years ahead of me. She knows everything about everyone in Greenwood back then. I asked if she remembered the two women with big bad hair and reputations to match in the arts and crafts house.

Janie's face lit up, in fact. "Shirley and what's her name?"

I told her about my visit to their doorstep and their civility that Sunday.

Janie listened and nodded. "Sure, that was the house." She paused in thought. "You know, I wouldn't call them prostitutes necessarily." She mulled a little further. "I'd say it was more just that they liked monetary gifts."

Shirley and her friend didn't wait for permission or the assigned route of others. For once, that one day in high school, I hadn't either. I had a chance to poke the boundaries of my life a little and get a glimpse of what was beyond the script. Did my life transform in that moment? Of course not. Back in the car, at the end of the afternoon, we drove back to the chamber of commerce and handed in our half-empty tubs of quarters. We all went home.

The encounter with Shirley and what's her name slipped into the back of my mind. Nothing much changed for me, certainly not what I considered the shame of my boy-free high school career. Yet more happened that day than I knew. I learned that volunteering offered more than sitting at home. When the right opening to step up for a cause came along—meaning one that would bring something extra to the table for me besides doing an institutionally approved good deed—the world could count on me. Something fundamental did occur that day, in fact. I ignored the givens set out by my family and town. I pushed back and did my own interrogation of reality. There was the ask to Shirley about a donation, of course, but the big ask was to myself. Was I going to take more steps to test the answers I'd been handed about my world? Yes, I was.

Chapter 2

In Which I'll Always Have Paris

ALONG WITH PHONE CHARGERS AND LOTS OF UNDERWEAR, vacationers tote to-do lists. Sometimes the agenda is an obvious no-brainer, other times more free-floating and hazily unsaid. When I was thirty-eight and headed to Paris, my agenda happened to be sex. Two kinds, to be specific. I wanted to have it with my husband, Gus, but I also wanted an easier coexistence with it as a dimension of life than I'd had lately as a dutiful-mother widget in Jackson's most uptight zip code. My prepping for France centered on projecting my dreams onto what I sensed was the upcoming willing French oxygen. I had faith in the prospect, in fact. I was Paris curious.

Fourteen years into marriage, Gus and I took pride in our solid, settled life—as bougie as they come, with two daughters, ages nine and five, a sugar cookie–yellow station wagon, and a weeklong Florida rental along C-30A in Walton County every July—yet were terrified that we had become so crate-trained. Paris sounded like a plan under the circumstances, which included, if not having lots of cash, at least a Visa with a not-small credit limit. We'd deal with paying it off later.

Paris beckoned. Along with the general Jackson, Mississippi, bragging rights for tackling the City of Light, there were its prospects for us as a couple. Our marriage was fine, but who isn't up for seeing if there's an even better? Parisian DNA promised an unfettered suggestiveness—for me, anyway. We targeted a date nine months out on the calendar and booked Mrs. Green, our daughter Molly's first-grade teacher whose side hustle was overnight babysitting for traveling parents. Nine months of anticipation began.

It spoke to how hyperadult and officious we thought we were that the first calendar window for the trip appeared to be a slot nearly a year off. Yet there was a side benefit to the clogged calendar. It meant more time to imagine Paris beforehand, which was half the experience anyway.

Through a dust layer on a high shelf, I found *Perspectives de France*, my worn, black-covered French 101 college textbook. Marcel Proust's cookie crumbs juiced his memory; cracking open the old freshman book did the same for me. My willing susceptible mind careened back to a weirdly sexually dreamier time in my life as an eighteen-year-old at my southern Baptist college. The lack of sex, nor any prospect of having it, had given me time to think and fantasize. Otherwise, my freshman off-hours passed in Baptist Student Union meetings and late-night runs with my suitemates for Peanut Buster Parfaits at Dairy Queen. With no chance of sex really materializing, I had ample time for fantasy. If I'd had something better to do, I wouldn't have.

Along with nearly two decades of dust mites, my eighteen-year-old freshman speculations floated up out of *Perspectives*. On the stationary bike at the workout center, I'd gasp and huff over all the French and related imagined scenarios I'd forgotten over the years. This included but was not limited to images of stubble-cheeked French men, groups of French men, and just a generalized knowing energy to wrap me instead of my real-life wristwatch and timetable. I started reading Paris guidebooks after supper while Kate and Molly had homework and baths.

I'd make the most of the coming five Paris days. On a map, I marked what streets were near the hotel I'd picked and x-ed our closest metro stop at Saint-Sulpice. I took ownership of the thought that Gus and I were going to be residents of the sixth arrondisse-ment, even if our five days were in a hotel room. Simultaneously, my anxiety roiled over leaving Kate and Molly. I drew up a will. I had Gus do the same.

"Why are you worried?" Gus asked. He wasn't.

"There have to be plans if something happens to us." I couldn't wrap my head around why Gus *wouldn't* fret.

"But if you're dead, you don't need to worry," Gus said. "You're gone." He flipped his hand over, showing an empty palm above his coffee and toast at the kitchen table to emphasize fate's unknowable nature.

I didn't buy it, nor could I convince myself that his argument was somehow a deceptively deep, Buddha-like response. Anyway, a lawyer friend drew up the wills. We signed. The trip packing began.

Departure morning arrived. Gus and I kissed the girls good-bye, leaving Mrs. Green with absurd reams of a micromanaged printout schedules for Kate and Molly. No wonder there was no regular room left over for more in my head.

Then, a mere one hour into the trip, changing planes in Atlanta, the promise of the vacation already blossomed. Gus unfolded his six-foot self out of the Jackson–Atlanta commuter plane, his gray sports jacket hanging over his forearm. I hoisted my carry-on of guidebooks on my shoulder and straightened my go-to black church skirt, which struck me as right for an overnight flight.

Once inside Hartsfield, I scanned the concourse. I had an agenda. As soon as I spotted a Delta uniform, I asked, "Excuse me. Where's the gate for Paris?" I wanted to hear myself say the words. Departure monitors were everywhere, of course. I asked a few more times anyway just to keep feeling the words on my lips.

Around eight the next morning, our flight landed at Charles de Gaulle. We were thick brained and jet lagged. The taxi driver lugged our suitcases out of his trunk and bullied us into overtipping him by fifty dollars—strange money, strange math. It took another night's sleep before we realized what he'd pulled. It was too late to matter.

Paris gleamed instantly.

Over espressos at an outdoor café table, we waited for the hotel room to be ready. Behind his wire rims, I watched Gus's eyes take in the stream of scarfed passersby flowing along the sidewalk in dark, muted coats and sweaters on that May morning. In Mississippi, the switch to Easter egg–hued springtime clothes had happened in April. Before us were Parisians in wool mufflers, black leather, and an unsmiling intensity. They strode by on the Left-Bank sidewalk with places to go as we watched.

"Is it what you thought it'd be?" I waved a pinch of my *pain aux raisins* as I asked.

Gus shook his head with an open mouth. I always loved to look at Gus caught up in wonder. All the passersby's jaded expressions accentuated how very unjaded he was in the café chair.

"Look at this," he said. He swished his hand around, and the corners of his eyes crinkled behind his wire rims. No one dressed and strode like this in Jackson, Mississippi, at ten thirty on a weekday or any other time, really. In happy disbelief, he shook his head, as his espresso turned cold. "I just didn't know." He fingered his saucer. "I didn't know it'd be so fucking French."

That pretty much sums up Paris. And the enthusiasm of Gus.

And just as I hoped, not just Paris shone. We did too. Our conversation seemed wittier. We felt smarter. Egged on by the city's glow, we sensed a new luster to us. I read Gus lines out loud from *French Lessons* by Alice Kaplan and kept saying "Je suis costaud," because in Kaplan's junior year exchange, that's what she thought her lover, briefly a student of insect extermination in Bordeaux, was probably muttering when he dropped off to sleep after sex. Kaplan thought he was saying "I am strong," but she later realized it was the phonetically adjacent "I'm still drunk." The passage was less about getting the translation right than how we repeated the syllables together. We needed a secret slogan, and we drafted Kaplan's punch line as our cue to arch our eyebrows and share understood smiles.

Meanwhile, on the metro, we kept a wordless lookout for Parisian neckwear champs, passengers who could flip their scarves into ad-lib, stylish insta-knots as the subway lurched. They'd do a mirrorless readjustment just before their stop.

I wished I could cut more of a figure myself than I did in the Ann Taylor pastels I'd packed. I bought a tangerine-and-scarlet Sonia Rykiel scarf at Galeries Lafayette, along with amber-lensed, rectangular sunglasses, which, looking back, did make me look like Bono, unfortunately. Gus bought a gray muffler from an open-air vendor along the Seine to add a Gallic touch to his matching gray sports coat.

We spent the equivalent of the monthly car note on a dinner of foie gras and lamb at the restaurant Taillevent. Before the trip, Gus had asked every guy he knew who'd ever been to Paris what to do about the haughty Taillevent sommelier he'd inevitably face. Gus had practiced what he was going to say, yet it turned out the sommelier's livelihood was based in part on humoring tourists.

"Of course," was the most intimidating words the tuxedoed steward said as he spun on his heels to bring the champagne.

At a round table near ours, an older American woman presided over a party that she seemed to be hosting. Her shoulders square and her French silky and effortless, she held court encircled by a half-dozen French male tablemates leaning in to catch her every word. As I strained to eavesdrop, the sole giveaway that she was American, to my rudimentary ear, was her flat-tongued vowels in the word or two of English that peppered her French conversation.

"Je suis arrivée de Cleveland qui est située à l'Ohio," I heard her say. What was her story? She managed fluency and Right-Bank looks with a navy windowpane Chanel-ish jacket, a chest-long strand of pearls that moved with stateliness as she talked, and salt-and-pepper hair looped in a refined—is my memory playing tricks?—French twist.

Tourists that we were, when Gus and I departed Taillevent, we shamelessly took our menu and wine label as souvenirs. Paid and tipped into nightly benevolence, the waiter beamed and delivered a warm farewell handshake. I buzzed with champagne, worldliness, and my racing thoughts over the sight of the wondrously at-ease American in navy blue enjoying her reign at her round table. I felt like a transformed person for having seen and spied on a life like hers.

French's mustard from the grocery store isn't very French, but its assured hue of yolk yellow is. That was the wall color in room 18, our quarters at the twenty-room Hôtel Le Saint-Grégoire. Our room was the result of all my months of guidebook reading. I decided for location, charm, and price, determining this was our place. Despite my months of pretrip map study, I hadn't fully grasped Left-Bank layout. Hôtel Le Saint-Grégoire's block was a bit out of the way. A fluorescent pharmacy was next door and the closest sidewalk café a street or so off. Yet our yolk-walled room had the bona fides to evoke a kind of Paris I'd imagined back in Mississippi. The room had a nineteenth-century honey-brown bureau made of faux bamboo and a fruitwood-framed oil of blousy white flowers in a compote. There was a florist vase of red roses as a welcome from the Saint-Grégoire on the bamboo chest. Each morning, I watched how the red petals shape-shifted overnight to open more. Gus and I morphed, too, our sense of possibilities stretching our rib cages to new dimensions. We could move in the big wide world, not just in the predictability of Jackson's regular carpool lanes and courtrooms. Gus and I co-opted the free-floating energy—which we were certain was in the Paris air—to get to believe in our momentarily dazzling selves. This applied to nothing in particular and to everything. Every night, I fluffed up the display on top of room 18's bamboo chest. I incorporated every day's afternoon accumulation: the slightly mashed Louvre Museum pamphlet, the half-folded copy of the day's *International New York Times*, fanned postcards from Giverny, and our Paris city map courtesy of the Galeries Lafayette. I'd tweak the bureau still life just so, reangling the Paris handouts to tell the day's story alongside the vase of morphing blooms.

As Gus and I made love, I imagined we were also somehow making love with everything the room and city symbolized to me. Paris pounded in my head. It was what I'd charted out during the girls' bath time for all those months, although Kate and Molly were no longer what I was thinking about. There was Gus's warmth, mine, and the creak of the bed. My exhilaration was a mix of us with the components of room 18: the transitory roses, the French yellow, and the third-floor peek of the sixth arrondissement outside the casement windows above 43 Rue de l'Abbé Grégoire.

We were intoxicated with what we were: inflated and dizzy. Isn't that a core truth of your exuberance over whom or what you love—how, when together, you adore how you feel inside yourself in a bubble of a moment? The fact was that Paris made me feel spectacular. I came to Paris expecting to broaden, curious to brush up against a sensuality I would never have owned up to while stirring casseroles, prissing through Jackson, and having nice married sex in Mississippi. I marshaled my packed-down secret hunger for sensuality and boldness to Paris. I wanted to be seduced and be a seducer in return. I drew a bead on Paris to take in its otherness, needing a swig of what I lacked. I pegged the city as a provider. There was neither a textbook nor guidebook for what I really craved, so I'd spent months conducting a one-off prep with the French textbook and Paris guidebooks to point me toward my ineffable. And for five days, it seemed to work.

On the last day, I found a tourist shop that sold the poster: Robert Doisneau's mass-marketed 1950 *Le Baiser de l'Hôtel de Ville*. The photo shows lovers in a hard sidewalk kiss as blasé pedestrians walk around them. The man's possessive arm folds across the back of his lover's cardigan, his fingers spread to claim her shoulder. Her mouth lifts up to his, her form positioned skyward as if rising to life's messy-haired dare. The couple's unselfconscious voltage seemed exactly what I'd been busy projecting onto the city. In truth, Doisneau's photo had a manufactured backstory: the shot was staged to run in *Life* magazine. When posters of the image eventually went up for sale in 1986, the woman sued Doisneau for a share of the royalties. Even so, for me, roiling insides were what I wanted, and that kiss delivered.

If I'd known her real story, maybe the Chanel-clad American from Taillevent might have burst my fascination bubble too. I didn't care. She served a mythic purpose for me, half due to my domestic overload, half due to my inner hope that the Paris trip would inflate me beyond my nice-enough everyday world somehow. I took that diner at Taillevent as my icon, a partaker of more. If I needed to believe in wider possibility for myself, I needed to believe that luster and lavishness swished and dangled from the mystery woman like her pearls. She represented wide expectations, how one gives life a big smack, as the poster couple kissing on command at the Hôtel de Ville.

I permitted Paris to change me—for those five days anyway. Yet I guess inevitably I couldn't remain that different person once home. First, I came to my senses and tossed the loser Bono sunglasses. Gus didn't waste much time when it came to my luck at knotting the Sonia Rykiel scarf. He took a look at the hopelessly un-French results of my labored finagling at wrapping the Paris scarf at my neck and said, "You know, when you tie it, it just kind of looks like a Cub Scout." He was right, actually. My touch was sad compared to the blasé metro-riding scarf artists.

Back home, Gus worked through his voicemails. I slipped my freshman French book back onto its hard-to-reach shelf. All that remained of the trip was the Visa balance and a stellar memory. That happens.

At age thirty-eight and in a mortgaged house of our own, I assumed I'd outgrown dorm-wall art. I taped the poster from the Marais tourist shop to the inside wall of my closet anyway. I wanted to hide its embarrassing tourist cheesiness from everyone but me. The poster was close to felony-level cliché if anyone saw it. In Jackson that carries weight, because a woman's taste, or lack thereof, is a guaranteed subject of scrutiny by a certain kind of woman. (If I know this, I must be that kind.) There was more to my secret souvenir, though. Heat glowed in my throat at the sight of the photo, of the man's one-handed clutch of the woman's shoulder and at how he twisted to press his mouth hard on hers.

Mornings while dressing for carpool, I'd stare at his determined fingers on her cooperating deltoid, fixing my eyes on the couple's multiple spots of contact. I stared as I yanked on my running shorts in the morning and my Old Navy pj bottoms at night. I stared as I buttoned up my white cotton shirt for a ten o'clock Tuesday Junior League meeting and my fallback black skirt for the eight forty-five Sunday service at church—the same skirt I wore on the Paris flight.

I wanted to believe in a life where the heat and heedlessness of the Doisneau couple happened.

In truth, I wanted to believe in a life where I could want something, anything, without finding an excuse to back away. I had it now, whenever I came in sight of the body-locked Paris kissers taped up in my closet or recollected how we took on Paris as a dreamy idea and pulled it off. You know what's said about always having Paris. We had the story of who we were while there. Inside my head—and inside my closet where the poster's still on display—Paris will always be closer than the actual two Delta planes and 4,694 miles away.

Chapter 3

Renovation

HOME REMODELING IS LIKE FINDING THE LOVE OF YOUR LIFE. IF
it happens to you all the time, something is wrong. I admit to three
renovations in my past. It's the follow-up step to falling for an old
house, and I'm a woman who loves too much when it comes to
tired houses with plumbing that coughs and wood floors that sigh.

My childhood home in Greenwood was a perfectly good ranch.
It had all the midcentury trappings: central air, a pine-paneled
den, and a concrete patio, where my parents' cookout smoke and
Andrews Sisters LPs crooned through the backyard air on Saturday
nights. If I now want a house mellowed by age, it's because that clean,
practical ranch was a contrarian breeding ground. After all, their
dream ranch house was what my parents sought after Mississippi
childhoods in turn-of-the-century uninsulated wood frames. I may
be dazzled by clapboard, high ceilings, and the charm signaled by
such, but they weren't. Where I spot character, they saw places that
deliver shivers in January and sweat slicks in August. The romance
of place only goes so far if everyone's prickly heat itches.

My family's house tastes swing like a pendulum from one generation to the next, but Gus's family steered straighter. They kept a
soft spot for old houses through generations. Gus was the son of
an eternal old-house optimist who cajoled his sons into multiple
father-son fix ups.

Gus's father led the boys in reroofing their newly purchased old
house near downtown Gulfport, Mississippi. As heat waves radi-
ated off the rooftop, their father supervised from the grass below.
He offered lots of wisdom while he sipped iced tea as his teenage

sons baked above. When the boys actually finished, woozy and light-headed, their father commented that their work looked a little sloppy. The boys came at him with their hammers until their mother broke up the family good times.

Gus's dad's next assignment was for the three sons to rewire the house. When a live wire shocked the oldest brother, the trio balked. Their father brightly urged them to look at the project not as a chore but as a chance to try something for free. He pointed out the benefits of electroshock therapy to psych inpatients: "Boys, all a little shock will do is settle your nerves."

I sought out older places the minute I boxed up my things and left the college dorm. I surveyed cheap, decaying rentals in Jackson to find the one oozing the most charm. It became a housewarming rite for my mother to go into shock each time she saw one of my series of chosen dilapidated hovels. At my first on West Street, I came home after work one Friday evening to find my mother on the duplex's mildewed front porch. Fear had frozen her into a statue, standing stiff like life-size porch folk art as cars roared along. I pulled her inside, and her speech eventually returned, enough to form a question: "Why can't you live in one of those nice new apartment complexes?" She talked up swimming pools and the chance to meet other postcollege rookies.

I kept quiet that I thought renting a new functioning apartment in a soulless complex was a failure of imagination. Even so, there was some truth to my mother's anxiety about my block. I'd hear news about drug and assault arrests in a tight radius around my duplex. I always wondered if my mother knew the names of streets in my vicinity to connect to the police stories too. As the sirens of ambulances and patrol cars wailed by outside, I was busy spending off-hours in my living room, refinishing the 1920s wood mantelpiece and floor baseboards. I must have tickled landlords by having nothing better to do with my time than upgrade the properties that they had let deteriorate for years.

My mother wasn't the only one dumbfounded by my taste for vintage quarters, which, after marriage, expanded to aging single-family houses. When Gus and I mulled buying our third, we brought an architect friend along. Later, the architect commented that his second visit didn't scare him nearly as much as the initial walk-through. "That first time, I kept thinking Bette Davis was going to fly around the corner any minute with a hatchet," he said.

My sense of the remodeling timetable is pretty standard. Demoing takes a week. Then icebreaker visits are paid by the plumber and the electrician before the concrete foundation is poured. The concrete pour is the first quick gratification day, unless a bulldozer is needed for the teardown. If a bulldozer is involved and you do not have a child, adopt one for the day. In our renovation no. 2, the bulldozer considerately waited to crank up until after school. The carpool grapevine was swift and effective. Soon our block was jammed with enough onlookers to look like the bank parking lot late Friday afternoon. Children dangled out the windows of SUVs, gobsmacked as the moaning bulldozer crunched through doomed walls.

Eventually comes framing, also high in instant gratification. Looking up at the rising lumber skeleton gives meaning to all the checks you're handing out on Fridays. As the frame comes into shape, whole rooms are birthed in an hour or so. You get the idea of what fifteen feet by twenty feet looks like and what a four-foot-wide hallway feels like.

Then it's time for electricians, plumbers, and the heating-cooling troop to stuff the pine bare bones with their pricey goods ahead of Sheetrocking. If you are in residence during your project, you will likely bottom out during Sheetrock week. White powder covers everything, including nasal cavities and dinner. Ten minutes of Sheetrock action equals ten years of dust accumulation—more dust than produced by any other known human activity.

While we were in the Sheetrock abyss of renovation no. 2, six-year-old Molly lost a tooth. I asked to see it and then watched it slip from my fingers to a floor dotted with about seven million crumbs of white Sheetrock, all the size of baby teeth. After tears and futile searching, we gave up and wrote a plea for mercy to the tooth fairy.

The tooth fairy, it turned out, was a good sport and took our word that a baby tooth lay somewhere among all the specks.

Remodeling swallows the rest of life. You are on standby to answer a running volley of questions from subcontractors who want stock numbers and name brands no later than yesterday because they didn't bother to ask until it was urgent. It's up to you to drop everything else since the train is moving.

If you don't come up with a confident answer, the subcontractor will. Neglect to voice a choice, and you will live with theirs, after all. They will make a decision casually and go to lunch with a clear conscience. You are left with their thumbs-up forever. In the final days of renovation no. 3, the countertop installers caught me in the car. On the telephone, they reported that they had cracked one of the ordered marble bathroom countertops and watched the electrician crack the other. He had tried to use it for scaffolding. Regrettably, the building-supply store had no more of the old-school oyster-white marble that we'd chosen. Yet the counter guys had a solution. Orange marble, they reported. In fact, the building store had an astonishingly deep inventory of it. Even as we were on the telephone, the counter guys had green-lighted the store to fabricate replacement counters to glow Juicy Juice orange in our bathroom forever. The swap was possible in a mere fifteen hours.

"That's okay, right?" the voice continued with pride.

But for every story of a wire cross, I can match you with a tale of a team member who went the second mile for our project. The landscaper drove me to my gum surgery. The contractor made sure we finished no. 3 on time by organizing a rogue painting squad instead of waiting for the previously hired house painters now running late. Membership on our painting detail waxed and waned. It seemed to include anyone near our zip code with a couple of spare hours and a light enough case of the d.t.'s to make holding a paintbrush semisteadily a possibility.

Yet our gratitude to all in the workforce pales in comparison to our debt to Steve, the carpenter who raised our cat from the dead on, coincidentally, Easter morning. For us it was Holy Week in more ways than one. Besides preparing for Easter, we'd finally managed to move into our rehabbed house no. 3. We'd survived the six-month-long renovation, our latest and, we believed, final remodeling job. We were out of money, emotionally shot, and elated all at the same time. Still, our new home, circa 1941, had room for not just us four but for my mother as well and for anything we could think up to do.

Looking back, Good Friday was the last time we'd seen our calico cat JD. She had been perched on the kitchen table, giving the stink eye to my cousin Alice's visiting Jack Russell terrier Lulu, down below on the new glossy oak floor. Lulu had stopped by that night along with Alice to see our new quarters. On Saturday, we unpacked more boxes, and at bedtime, in the five-second lapse between when my head hit the pillow and falling asleep, I thought about JD. She'd never asked for food all day. When Easter dawned and JD was not scolding me at the kitchen door for breakfast, I knew she was in trouble.

Downstairs, I heard the faint meow in the backyard. Aha. She was outside. I stepped into the morning cool, looking under the carpenter's workbench, still on site along with the temporary orange utility pole. No JD.

I heard her again. A faint meow, coming from inside the house this time.

I went back inside. No cat.

I repeated this a few times, hearing the far-off mew in the yard, then, once I was out in the morning air, inside the house. Then the facts sunk in. JD wasn't outside, nor was she inside. She was within the new wall of the house.

Sure enough, a second-floor door to the central-air closet was slightly ajar when I checked. A cat might make a snap judgment that this was a great hidden cranny to distance herself from Lulu. I'd found JD's point of entry into the bowels of the house but saw no sign of her. Her yowl was audible, though.

I called the carpenter Steve at home about 8:00 a.m. on Easter. He threw on clothes and arrived within fifteen minutes, a feat even for a nineteen-year-old guy. He shimmied into the air duct between the first and second floor. "Yeah, I see her," he called out.

Apparently once she'd hidden in the second-floor AC closet, JD had trotted along the air duct's fluffy length of pink insulation, drifting deeper into the unknown and farther away from the offense of Lulu's existence. The duct, however, dropped off into an empty vertical wall cavity. JD's pink insulation pathway turned floorless, an unsupported flap over the two-story empty shaft. When JD strolled to the air duct's end, she'd wafted down into the empty shaft on her little Aladdin-like tuft of rosy pink insulation. She'd likely been resting on her fire-resistant tuffet since late Good Friday.

As JD yammered, we braced ourselves to rip out the just-completed den Sheetrock. I sighed, giving one last look at the pristine lemon walls with their loud, fresh Benjamin Moore smell.

"What about if we go in like this?" Steve suggested. Instead of bashing the Sheetrock, Steve walked over to the built-in cabinet that backed up to the shaft where JD was. The entire cabinet came out when he pulled it just so. Steve knew things.

The new wall was spared so far, but JD wasn't. The cabinet-free void was still far above JD, complaining at the shaft's bottom. We stared at the empty darkness as her outraged meows flew up. Next thing I knew, Steve had one of my ankles, Gus the other, and I was spelunking into the black hole, head first. A second later, still hanging upside down, JD and I locked gazes as blood sloshed into my upside-down head.

In true cat form, she kept her dignity despite thirty-six hours in her pit. She was never one to gush. JD trained her beautiful Coke-bottle-green eyes on me, in whose arms she had purred for sixteen years, and let out a withering rebuke. I clutched her as Steve and Gus reeled us back up by my ankles. Once returned to the light, I could swear she rolled her eyes when she took a look at the three of us, her slow tardy excuse for a rescue squad.

No Bible reader can miss the Good Friday to Easter parallel on our hands—from entombed to triumphant. We had much to celebrate. Yet JD's trial is also a parable about the life-draining, life-changing choice to attempt home renovation. The cat plunged into the unknown. She fell through space, and her whole life went in limbo for what seemed like an absurd, irrational length of time. Then she emerged into a sunlit room, and her hard knocks were over.

The same applied to us as dejected, exasperated renovators, who walked in one day and suddenly saw our project reality at long last. Our home was bright with pride and paint. By the end of our renovation, we were as shaken and crotchety as the hostage JD. Yet we lived through it and were soon willing to admit it might have been worth it after all.

And also like JD, we'd pause, though, before ever poking too far around an old house again.

Chapter 4

A Crack in the Floor

MY HUSBAND AND I ONCE OWNED A 1932 YELLOW STUCCO HOUSE
on what turned out to be a subterranean stretch of Yazoo clay.
Neighbors and friends were kind enough to bring welcome muf-
fins, a philodendron, and—this being Jackson homeownership—the
contact info of a church minister who did house-foundation work
weekdays.

When a bulge erupted in our front-hallway oak floor and the
Sheetrock cracked in vertical rivulets, we telephoned the minister.
Let's call him the Reverend Gerald Sims Junior. It turned out the
Sims family had a trademark legacy. Like his father, the Reverend
Gerald Sims Senior, Reverend Sims Junior preached on Sunday
and repaired clay-cracked foundations throughout town during
the week.

You have to question Jackson founder Louis LeFleur's site-picking
judgment. Millions of years before the fur trader opened his post
in 1792 on the bluff of the Pearl River, the city's fate was geologi-
cally sealed as one of the lousiest spots, besides a Pacific cliffside, to
build. It's the presence of montmorillonite, the offending mineral
in Jackson's clay, which sets house foundations in town to roiling
and cracking.

Maybe perching his enterprise on the bluff above the mosquitoes
and Pearl floodlands was a solid trade-off for gooey soil initially. But
buildings with more ambition and mortar followed LeFleur's log
quarters. Once the size of houses swelled, so did the foundations,
unfortunately.

In 1948, Yazoo clay punked Frank Lloyd Wright when he designed a dream house for Edith and Willis Hughes. Wright had earlier made his reputation when his iconic Imperial Hotel withstood the 1923 Tokyo earthquake. But then Wright came to Jackson, where 7.9 on the Richter scale in Tokyo turned out to be less of a test than Yazoo clay. Wright's low-slung Jackson hill hugger was built in fits and spurts between 1950 and 1954 as the Hugheses' oil business fluctuated. Word was that the three-thousand-square-foot concrete house—the family named it Fountainhead—started to crack before the Hughes clan spent their first night. Eventually, a section of the Fountainhead floor broke, sinking nineteen inches down. The roof peak split. Rain poured in. (Also, Wright insisted air-conditioning was only necessary if you didn't have a genius architect to configure cross breezes correctly—no AC needed for the new homeowners. Not eager to melt, subsequent owners retrofitted the home with AC.)

Reverend Sims arrived at our house (a few blocks from the Wright house) with his crew of deacons who addressed each other as brother. The team bent down and into the crawl space to get to work twisting our home back straight.

From the kitchen, I heard Reverend Sims three feet beneath my tennis shoes as he directed one of the deacons to coax a new piling into place below.

"Brother Edward? To the left." Reverend Sims's voice seeped up. "Brother Phillip? Over there." By late afternoon, the crew reemerged in the carport. Reverend Sims squinted in the daylight in his muddy, zipped coveralls. All was well again, he said.

"You know, a house is no better than its foundation." He was talking to me, but his delivery sounded like strong words to a congregation. It felt a little accusatory, in fact, although Reverend Sims had a kind smile above his gray goatee. I could see that the minister's Sunday and weekday work weren't totally at odds. In both capacities, he took on drift, either the human kind or house movement caused by clay. Clay was likely easier to fix.

Our hallway was mended. As Reverend Sims had said, all was well. Ten years passed. Then the Yazoo clay shifted once more. When the hairline crack in the kitchen counter first started, I overlooked it. Then it widened to vein size and made a sure trek across the shiny midnight-black stone surface—same for the bulge that split the planks in the wood floor below.

To tell the truth, both cracks had been growing unnoticed—probably brightly and willfully unnoticed by me—for quite a while. The fix was too big for Reverend Sims and the deacons to manage by solely nudging a new wood piling or shim into place from below. My husband and I hired a man with a jackhammer. The kitchen floor was shot. Not long after, so was our marriage. We sold the house. You can fight nature only so far, and then it's time to accept what's happening, going along with the earth's awful, wondrous rumbles.

Chapter 5

The Rubble of My Marriage, Hidden by Katrina's

HURRICANE KATRINA CAME ALONG AT A STRANGELY APPROPRIATE time for me. Its shattered lives and lost homes fell right in line with how my life was going at the moment. In the midst of divorcing after twenty-three years of marriage and two children, a process that had left my own life in tatters and my family house gone, I viewed the ninety-thousand-square-mile disaster as a public-scale match for my private misery. What's more, the poststorm frenzy here in Mississippi allowed me to hide in public, which I appreciated because I was not in the market for others' pity. I had self-pity enough to do the job.

In the storm's wake, even upstate Mississippi was in chaos: no power for weeks, shelters full of displaced people, roofs torn, and trees down. My school (I was a high school French teacher in a Jackson suburb) was expected to stay closed until the power returned, but then the state highway patrol requested that our area schools remain shut indefinitely to reduce traffic on US 49, the 150-mile corridor to the coast.

With most of the state's residents stuck at home with no work, gas, or electricity, I felt relieved not to have to participate in normal life. And the fact that everyone in my community was focused on the hurricane losses instead of my personal devastation doubled my relief.

The concern of others is easier to accept for turns of fate like illness or the death of loved ones. But there's humiliation in divorce, an unshakable sense of fault and inadequacy, as if you failed to grasp some essential point in setting up your dominoes long ago. And for my part in this failure I did not want awkward hugs or baked goods or Hallmark cards.

Thanks to Katrina, I did not get them. A single chicken casserole was all that arrived when I moved into my postdivorce house, a sign of just how upside down things were during those weeks in Mississippi, a place where women generally stockpile frozen chicken tetrazzini and chocolate soufflés to thaw and deliver at the first sign of trouble in their ranks.

A year later I had an operation, and friends kept me in pork tenderloins and red velvet cake for five weeks. But during that earlier hard time, as Katrina pounded its way through and my just-divorced self reeled, I thought about a scene from *The Good Earth*, when during the 1911 Chinese revolution, Luise Rainer's character flattens herself against the side of a building as a stampeding mob roars by.

The crowd roared by me as well, its focus pointed appropriately south, instead of descending upon and catering to the floundering divorcée in their midst by offering a nighttime ride to this, an extra ticket to that. There weren't even the regular social functions that might expose me to the murmured condolences I so hoped to avoid; public areas throughout Jackson were filled with storm victims and Red Cross workers and, in the case of the state coliseum grounds, hundreds of evacuated dogs and cats.

My own new house filled, too. A New Orleans friend telephoned from his French Quarter grocery store, asking if his wife and daughter could stay with me. We introduced ourselves as we unloaded their luggage. Tillie, their Border collie, slept on the floor, and their surprise friend Billy managed in the brown chair in the den.

As the days passed, I continued to personalize the tragedy to suit my own needs, to view the storm as a metaphor for my life and current circumstances, though it wasn't insensitive detachment that fueled my narcissism. The Mississippi coast had been my home on and off through life, so I found it natural to blend the public and the private loss, synchronizing my sadness for myself with the sadness I felt for those in a place that had been my home.

I spent much of my childhood in Pass Christian, where the storm surge blasted through at about thirty feet, wiping out much of the town. My namesake Aunt Ellen once had a pecan farm north of town and later a ranch house on Second Street.

The coast is where I had my first cigarette, Shirley Temple, and daily newspaper beat. I attended First Presbyterian Church in Gulfport, where my in-laws filled three pews. My husband and I married on the wooden porch of our just-purchased shotgun house near Pass Christian.

To my besieged sense of self, it seemed oddly logical that these landmarks of my past had been ravaged and obliterated, now that my expectations for life had blown away, too. Not that I spent all of my time wallowing in this kind of melodrama instead of helping out. As an able and concerned human being, I was capable of both wallowing and helping out. What woman doesn't multitask? So within a day or so after the body search had been called off, I was in a coast-bound van with six fellow church parishioners, all of us hoping to lend a hand.

As our van headed toward the Gulf, the degree of damage along US 49 worsened every twenty minutes. The leftover coffee in our cups cooled and our small talk diminished as we took in what surrounded us. About ninety minutes north of the Gulf, roadside pines teetered at forty-five-degree angles, tilted by hours of hurricane-force wind. Fifteen miles inland, stripped and flattened pine trees stretched away from both sides of the road like piles of pretzel sticks.

A few minutes later, we turned in to the grounds of Coast Episcopal School in Long Beach, a few miles from the beach, where the state Episcopalians and Lutherans were running their joint relief effort. The electricity was still out, and part of the gym's roof had been ripped off by the wind. But under all the debris, the school apparently was fine as a supply center, clinic, and sleeping space for volunteers.

It wasn't until we pulled off the blacktop, when I saw a row of surviving pecan trees planted in a straight line as if in an orchard row, that I realized where we were: the school had been built on the site of my Aunt Ellen's former pecan farm. Which also meant that the pink shotgun house where my husband and I had married twenty-three years earlier was on the next road over. Or had been.

In the school's dim entryway, still decorated with Welcome Back posters from the start of school two weeks before, about ten priests from the area, their own churches demolished, had gathered for an organizational meeting. Several dozen local Episcopalians were present, too, everyone in baseball caps, T-shirts, shorts.

Before long we all moved into the school library for a 10 a.m. Communion service. One large window across the room provided a little light, along with the two white altar candles on the study-hall table.

The Book of Common Prayer's Communion service has always soothed me, inspiring me to see the possibility of something larger and beyond myself, which I especially needed right then. The moment that feels most rich with potential is when I'm awaiting my turn for the priest to hand me the wafer. The separate pieces—the music, the voices, a turn of phrase, and the smooth wood of the altar rail—swirl together into a kind of mystical transcendence that rarely fails to move me. It becomes more than the sum of its parts and that stirs me. Because of this moment, I never turn down a Communion service, and I especially awaited this one.

I don't remember the Bible reading except for the fact that I of course found great identification with it. Then the service moved on to the Prayers of the People, and when the current catastrophe came up, several people started sniffling. A woman directly behind me sniffled especially hard. As the priest prayed for the survivors, her sniffling broke into a series of quick arrhythmic gasps.

This irritated me. But why? How could I possibly feel irritated by the suffering of people who had lost so much? In an out-of-body way, my meanness intrigued me. And I realized my kindness was damaged. I had become the sort of woman who probably strikes others as "hardened," someone who goes about life grim faced and tense mouthed, believing herself to be saddled with mistakes, bad luck, and bitterness. Somehow her potholes aren't a surprise to her or anyone else. Hardened women all had a divorce under their belt, I thought.

I was glad to be a Katrina foot soldier, handing out insulin and water and helping to clean out the school gym, and I felt good, I suppose, about my efforts. But more revealing to me that day was how resentful I was of this woman's sanctioned public grief, and how jealous of these arrangements and concern on her behalf.

True, I had claimed I didn't want any pity or attention and was grateful to have been spared such efforts. But I saw then that I had confused my own avoidance of pity for disdaining sympathy or concern in general, when actually I craved it, or at least I craved something.

I didn't get it in that makeshift church. And I don't want to claim that I found it through anything as good and as noble as suddenly forgetting my own troubles by throwing myself into the service of others.

No, where it happened was in the middle of the Long Beach shopping center parking lot, where I later stood amid acres of surplus donated clothing, a three-foot-deep expression of the world's good wishes stretching out before me, thousands of T-shirts and nightgowns and pants and sweatshirts flown in for the displaced. Far too many ever to give or take away, the donations baked unclaimed on the asphalt.

This massive collection of goods wasn't directed at me, and I needed none of it. But the world's lavish concern had created this sea of clothing—there was a surplus of that free-floating compassion to go around as well, and I drank it in. No humiliating words of pity or condolence, no awkward pats or hugs. Just the knowledge that so many cared and took action, however disconnected or redundant or futile. And maybe I slipped one pale-blue T-shirt out of the acreage just for me as a reminder. There were more than enough. My new T had a Bacardí rum logo and trademark dank smell, sent by an anonymous someone to support an anonymous recipient, who turned out to be squirrely me. It was perfect.

Standing in that parking lot, I felt something small but fundamental shift in me, and my life finally started to move along again.

Chapter 6

Lessons in the Past Tense

ONLY IN MISSISSIPPI DO YOU TEACH BECAUSE $28,000 AND FREE
Blue Cross sounds good. I was a rookie in the classroom and at
being a forty-eight-year-old divorced mom. Three weeks into my
second year at Brandon High, Katrina hit. The storm was the shove
I needed to admit to myself that I wanted to return to my former
work as a journalist. The proof was my envy of reporters getting
to write the story of the decade as the community climbed back. I,
meanwhile, had let myself be seduced by a teacher's fat paycheck
and that 3:30 p.m. dismissal. Resigning would be shoddy—if I did,
there would be no French teacher at all—and it's not as if I had any
journalism job waiting. I'd job hunt when the school year ended—a
mere 173 days off. I checked the countdown no more than three
times every day, tops.

Antoinette, a New Orleans tenth grader, joined my French II class
after evacuating to her relatives' Brandon home with her mother.
(I've changed her name.) She had a tight, worried gaze. Touched by
the panic in her eyes, I put a hand on her back the first morning.

"Sit by me," I said. "Follow what we're doing, and see if your class
was doing about the same."

She folded into a front-row desk, four feet away. Her shoulders
loosened slightly, but her eyes stayed on me, never letting go of my
face, not even to glance at her classmates. Antoinette, with short,
side-parted hair, wore skinny jeans and a ribbed turtleneck. The outfit may or may not have been to her taste, since her supply of clothes
had come as donations. Her own clothes were lost in New Orleans,

where she'd gone to a well-known historically African American parochial girls' school.

I always started class the instant the bell quieted. Take the offense, seasoned teachers advised me. My copy of the teacher edition of *Discovering French* jutted at my hip in an aggressive attempt to show authority.

"Aujourd'hui nous sommes à la page soixante-trois. Alors, commençons," I said, telling students to turn to page 63. I tried to bore my gaze into those looking.

My bell-to-bell French drills with the too-big, antsy class weren't because I was conscientious, but because it was the only tactic I could figure out to possibly stay in control. That, of course, is the real aim in running a school. Talk yourself blue about nurturing a passion for learning, but the truth is, an administrator's idea of a crack teacher is one who keeps students subdued and in a busy-work headlock that chokes out all potential chaos. What's optimal is keeping the school machine running smoothly and silently. (Another veteran teacher pass-along: New teachers shouldn't smile until Thanksgiving, or the students will wipe the floor with you.)

Our class was ahead of Antoinette's old one. "We didn't have this," she whispered at the end of her first class.

"Don't worry. We'll work it out after you get settled," I said.

"I don't know how to do this," she'd report every morning about her homework in the thirty seconds before the room filled in subsequent days. Then the bell would sound, and Antoinette evaporated from my focus. I had to stay on top of the group for the next ninety minutes. To me, the restless, bored class felt no more than a hair's breadth away from chaos if I didn't role-play a teacher who had control of her class while the clock ticked off the minutes.

"Activité A, s'il vous plaît."

The next bell would eventually ring. Another second period muddled through.

After a month, Antoinette was still lost in class. Her frantic, searching eyes came into the room ahead of her body. Her face's rigidity never loosened throughout the period. (My high school ran on four ninety-minute classes instead of the old six-class, fifty-minute model. That was so the administration only had to contend with students loose in the hall changing class four times daily, not six.)

Her hair pulled back into a nape bun, Antoinette wore lots of earth-shade turtlenecks and jeans. I collected a grocery sack of overflow from Kate's and Molly's closets.

"See if you could use any of these," I said.

Next day, Antoinette returned the paper sack full. I don't think she said why. I wonder now. Our talk must have been cut short by another student's louder attention-sucking hijack, which trumped Antoinette's subdued tone if I was to keep the class train running. I think back on Antoinette as a series of quick prebell exchanges, the only attention I gave her. My mission was to stay one step ahead of the second-period group, which I saw as a collective version of a waiting IED.

"Let's get serious about catching you up," I said to Antoinette in November. "What's the best time to work—before or after school?"

Neither, she said. Her bus arrived just in time for school and departed about one minute after the three-thirty bell. That was correct. The buses were precisely timed to whisk students away to circumvent after-school trouble on campus. Could we work during my planning time, first period? She shook her head. She had algebra and couldn't miss.

So I never sat down with her. She kept turning in nearly blank tests. The week that we started the *passé composé*, I handed back the graded tests, including Antoinette's nearly blank one. As usual, she reported that her old school hadn't covered this.

"Antoinette," I said, "nobody in here had the past tense until this week. This is what we're doing—you and everyone else." I didn't hide my exasperation. I wish I had now.

Next day, instead of sitting by me, she took a desk in the back of the room, slumping into the seat. She had the protected, low forma-tion of a Gulf live oak with a horizontal, hunkered shape, the live oak's survival adaptation against the wind's assault in a hurricane. I never called on Antoinette out loud unless I was certain she knew the answer. Of course, that meant I rarely did.

I checked with the guidance office. Antoinette was assigned to the cute counselor, who wore miniskirts and a denim jacket and was always tossing her long honey hair over her shoulders. She defied the teacher cliché of tired mom pants and cheerful novelty sweaters. The cute counselor was unsurprised at my report that Antoinette was languishing in second period.

"I'm trying to get her in at Mental Health," she said with a flip of her cute locks. "Her depression has gotten so severe."

It hadn't hit me. What I'd been watching with dense irritation was a tenth grader moving closer to imploding, one day to the next. Exactly how important was French II in Antoinette's chaos, after all? I myself didn't give a rip about French II either. Antoinette's life had disappeared in a day. To make things worse, the counselor reported, her mother had returned to work in New Orleans, leaving Antoinette behind with her Mississippi cousins.

My countdown until the last day of school was coming closer to the end. I assigned everyone in French II to write a brief report on an aspect of French culture. Coco Chanel and Versailles were favorite topics.

"Can I do something about New Orleans?" Antoinette asked.

On report day, she headed to the front with her poster. I sensed curiosity in the room over what the always-silent classmate would say. Antoinette held up her board, pasted with a printout image of a Bloody Mary–red Quarter townhouse with a traditional iron-lacework balcony.

"This is the French Quarter—where the white people lived," she said. "It stayed dry. It was the Black neighborhoods that flooded."

She looked at her classmates with a confiding smile, knowing and bitter. The class had snapped to attention over the tight, quiet fury in her voice. She paused a moment.

"That's what they planned," she said more softly.

No one said anything, not any of the white students, who made up the overwhelming majority of the class, nor any of the few other Black students in the room.

I didn't debate what she said either. I could have argued that what happened in New Orleans was callous but not specifically calculated. I could have argued that it showed an indefensible lack of concern but not a working conspiracy. In fact, what happened in New Orleans in Katrina was pretty much the equivalent of my approach to being Antoinette's teacher.

I've checked Facebook. I want to find Antoinette there, to see that she's okay, back in New Orleans with her mother. Out of the dozen or so possible Antoinettes I found, there is not one I can believe is her, no confirmation so I can check off that Antoinette is now smiling and restored.

Back in French II that day, Antoinette finished her New Orleans presentation. She walked back to her desk in the back of the room and refolded herself into the low slump at her desk where she'd weathered the year. Her expression was empty, her shoulders sunken with resignation. I looked at the clock. Only six minutes until the bell. One more report would get us to the end, I calculated.

"Who's next?" I asked.

Chapter 7

The Divorcée's French Class

I ONCE SPENT TWO YEARS AS A HIGH SCHOOL FRENCH TEACHER. I took the post because I was divorcing and needed a paycheck. The school took me even though I had no teaching experience because, under Mississippi law, if a school is hard up for a teacher, it can hire anyone the state designates an "expert citizen."

For some reason, I found the citizen part personally touching. It conveyed a sense of responsibility packed along with my new, free Blue Cross insurance card and pad of pink detention slips. Yes, though I felt failed and foolish starting over at forty-eight, my credentials were a consolation prize. They said I was an expert when it came to French drills for ninth graders, even if not an expert at staying married.

I quit in 2006 and went back to my old day job of journalism. But not long afterward, a friend asked me to give French lessons to an acquaintance of hers. The woman had just divorced. As part of rebooting her life, she wanted to learn French. I reflexively said yes.

She came to my house the next Saturday morning. Her name was Susan. She was fifty-three, with brown hair brushing her shoulders and a job dealing with cellphone towers. I taught her the ABCs and how to introduce herself. I found myself asking her about her divorce and telling her about mine. The next Saturday, we practiced "ça va?" and "merci." I had more divorce questions for her and some thoughts to share with her about mine.

This was more fun than the high school job. Word spread about the French lessons. More asked to come. I organized classes at my dining-room table and named my business Le Salon Français. Soon,

I had four weekly classes coming to my house, one on Thursday afternoons and three on weeknights.

It was time to buy textbooks. My school district, like most in the area, still used the 1997 edition of *Discovering French*, full of white teenagers like Isabelle and Jean-Paul, outdated even then, who partied down in pleated pants, shaking their manes of moussed hair to the beat of their Walkman cassettes. Skits on the accompanying videos featured teenagers' soirées, throbbing with eighties pop on the record player.

Mississippi perpetually stands near the bottom in public school spending, and our time-frozen textbook reflected it. It seemed like the rest of the country was through with this publication, judging from the number of copies I found for sale online. I could buy them for $2.95 each. Lots of additional used *Discovering French* paraphernalia were out there. I presume they were semifenced goods from French teachers in other poor states like Louisiana and Nevada. Some teacher there must have been quietly liquidating the contents of her room's book closet to sweeten her budget for a summer trip. One week, an extra set of the videos came up on eBay. I was outbid, interestingly. I have to wonder who else could possibly have wanted them.

I don't think people came to my classes for *Discovering French*. I think I was drawing in other wrecked people via spiritual attraction. Most of my students were women in their fifties, getting over one kind of trauma or another, as I was. Among sixteen students, there were seven divorces, including one that involved coming out of the closet; a few breakdowns; two murders of loved ones; cancer; rehab; and caretaker responsibilities for a bedridden sister.

Did I mention that our lessons paused for two weeks for me to have an emergency craniotomy, or that my dog, Sonny, was dying of cancer himself under the dining-room table?

We progressed from pronunciation to the gender of nouns to the present tense. We paused to hear one another's updates. No matter if we told time in lesson 4 or play-ordered sandwiches in lesson 9, we always had time for the latest when it came to someone's divorce, child-custody situation, criminal appeal, or change of medication.

To tell the truth, the foreign-language gene was recessive in my salons. Sometimes we'd cover the same material three weeks in a row, and it didn't seem any more familiar to the participants the third time than the first. After a year, we'd made it only to page 106, lesson 15. That was where my French I class at my high school would be by January.

My oldest student was eighty-three. Her name was Sis. The class wasn't easy for her because her hearing aid crackled a lot. One week I realized that I was turning textbook pages for her during class. I did it as automatically as I used to cut the meat on my daughters' plates, never slowing the conversation.

But my students weren't discouraged by their progress. Nor was I.

"Guess what I did yesterday," the eighty-three-year-old Sis asked me one day. "I counted the cars that drove down the street—in French. I counted to 126!" She wore little round black-framed glasses like a hip architect and a pressed white blouse. She smiled and lifted her chin. "Of course, I've always said French things to myself. I've had a spiritual reading, and the lady said I've lived several lives in France. That's why it's all so natural for me."

One student said, "I'm dreaming in French now." This was great news, though maybe a little curious, since her class had a repertory of exactly twelve verbs and hadn't gotten to sentences yet.

Another responded, "When I pray in the mornings, I do it in French."

But perhaps the most rewarding response was that of a woman—let's call her Elaine—whose French bliss was even simpler. All she had to do was say *un jus d'orange*. She said it over and over. The sensuality of the syllables transported her. She'd throw back her chin as her eyes rolled back in her head, halfway home on the Meg Ryan spectrum of pleasure. French phonetics can do that.

When I declared my marriage over and myself a French teacher, I figured all I had to do was stay a mere thirty minutes ahead of my students to come off as proficient enough to teach them. That worked for ninth graders, but in adult education, I don't kid myself that I know anything more than my classes in terms of the core curriculum, which is this: French can save you. So can particle physics, furniture refinishing, or any other venture you take up while the world spins on. Compartmentalize a spot in your reeling head, and that little space becomes a refuge, full of possibility. At least for a one-hour-a-week lesson, anyway.

Chapter 8

Daffodils

IN THE FALL OF 1908, A HURRICANE GUSHED THROUGH MY GREAT-grandparents' farm in the Mississippi Delta. The farm was 250 miles inland from the Gulf of Mexico, a sea that until then had only come their way as a pretty pastel-tinted postcard or two in the mail.

The Gulf arrived as a package of fury that day, destroying the cotton crop and bankrupting the farm. Forty years after the Civil War marked the end of their parents' cotton farms on the east side of the state, Ann and her husband, Frank, saw their small Reconstruction next chapter pelted to steamy shambles.

It was typical of Ann's plotline that there was yet another turn after the farm's foreclosure. An elderly uncle in Nashville died and left her money. She took the cash and bought another patch of land just down the road from the repossessed one. At sixty-one, Ann started over again and bought the new farm in her own name. I love that part of the story.

Ann and Frank spaced sticks of tiny pecan saplings along one acre and built a dogtrot house in the middle of the patch of pecan twigs. Calling it an orchard or even much of a house at that point was overdoing it. The site fronted a dirt road and cypress bayou. The house of Ann's birth was built by the hands of enslaved workers. That Monroe County home had been torched by Ohio troops right after her father was shot and killed by them in the front yard in February 1864 as the family watched. I tell myself maybe the enslaved workers of her parents left with the Ohio soldiers. I also tell myself that Ann, the heroine of this story, was a mere sixteen-year-old daughter without much agency herself inside her privilege. (Of course I set up these flimsy pillars for the purposes of this story because the history that comes down to me overwhelms me otherwise.)

On her new land, Ann settled into her dogtrot in the fledgling pecan patch of the Delta frontier. (Unlike the assumed cliché, the Delta didn't open for substantial homesteading until after the Civil War. It was only after quinine was found to be a cure for malaria in the late nineteenth century that settlers migrated in substantial numbers from settled areas.)

Ann planted daffodils. She loved them all—early, sweet-smelling narcissus, late yellow King Alfred types: Campernelle, Pheasant's Eye, Butter and Eggs, White Cheerfulness. Neighbors offered spare bulbs up to a sister flower lover. Ann indulged in actually paying money for a few special bulbs by mail, a massive extravagance at the time. Time passed, and Ann's daffodils signaled the new growing season every year.

Daffodils in the crisp sun signaled a four-week warning that cotton planting was coming. March daffodils fit a farm like May rain and August heat. Yellow daffodils shone as heedlessly as hope in spring. Neither reality nor a plow could touch dreams or a field as early as March. The surrounding empty, rich acres begged for cotton. The orchard was carpeted in shining yellow. A turquoise sky glinted through the net of pecan branches in the bracing cold. Teetotalers that Ann and Frank were, it was intoxicating.

Before too long, planting season came. A hangover seeped in from the hopeful March mental spree. Giddiness didn't last forever. Work came with each morning's sunrise. The crop was planted. The daffodil blooms faded, and foliage shriveled.

The daffodils disappeared for another year. Reality took their place. By May, it was possible to believe in too much rain, drought, pests, or low prices. Spring flowed into summer, which lapsed into fall. The crop played itself out, for better or worse. Hopefully the cotton was passable. Occasionally it was astounding, though good farmer form limited gloating to the loaded superstitious response "We did all right." The crops were picked, the books settled, and

December set in. As sure as December, the green daffodil foliage poked through the ground once more.

For twenty years, Ann's daffodils opened the Sunflower County farm's annual cycle. Then came the Great Flood of 1927. At age eighty, Ann knew foreboding as trouble approached. This disaster featured neither Ohio soldiers nor a foreclosing banker. Fate was rolling her way in the form of murky floodwater coming from forty miles to the west. The flow ate out mile after mile of the Delta as it continued roaring out of the levee rupture near Greenville. Deltans packed belongings, raised beds onto blocks, and nailed rafts together as word arrived that the water was on its way in a few hours.

At Ann's farm, the last-minute push was on. The river water was coming in three hours. After eight decades of life switchbacks, Ann had a clear idea of what she'd choose to save this time. She picked the daffodils. If she could keep the daffodils and what they represented, she could deal with losing the rest. Out came the clumps, smelling sweet of the black Sunflower County loam.

As the Mississippi seeped closer, she loaded the bulbs in burlap feed bags, hung them from the smokehouse rafters, and evacuated another home. With the daffodils dangling dry overhead, Ann beat the flood, and the family spent the next three weeks packed in a relative's house in Inverness—the man ran the town gas station—with other refugees. (My mother, then twelve, loved getting to evacuate to town and the fact that since the teachers fled town secretly on a train at night, school was out. She also remembered her grandmother Ann and her own mother fretting over cooking for their cousin-in-law host—they felt menu pressure because townspeople were used to eating meat at every meal, the women worried.)

The foul floodwater started to recede. The family returned home to a forlorn turf of silt and snakes. They replanted the crop. Ann pulled the bulbs down from the rafters, and they went back in the orchard ground where they belonged.

Ann's knack for hot- and cold-running fate hadn't stopped. By the fall of 1927, the cotton crop turned out to be one of the best ever, thanks to the silt-enriched soil. The flood had turned the fields, at least for that year, into something along the order of "the richest land this side of the valley Nile," to steal Tennessee Williams's line about Delta dirt from *Cat on a Hot Tin Roof*.

The daffodils morphed the next year too. Whether it was the boost from the silt or separating the bulbs inadvertently when she had pulled them up, the daffodils spilled out wider and brighter, an orchard-sized, sun-suffused March carpet.

There is a photograph of Ann, late in her life on the back porch of her dogtrot house in the pecan trees—the onetime seedlings matured into crop-bearing, lacy trees. She wears a pale print dress and a serious press to her lips created from eighty-nine years of holding out her plate to see what time and place were serving her that day.

I think about her last years as she reflected on all she'd witnessed. I'd like to think there was remorse for her family's—my family's—crime of slavery. Is that likely in 1920s Mississippi? No, it wasn't. I do know, though, what she did with the earth on which she lived when the choice became hers to make in 1927 and her name was on the property deed. Her choice is on display to this day in the March field of blinding yellow in Sunflower County.

Eras end. You eye choices, such as they are, or at least how you see them. Ann planted some daffodils. Her pick of a first step for a new start doesn't strike me as a bad one.

Part 2

Steps Taken . . . or Not

Chapter 9

Volunteering (2)

IN THE FALL OF 1974, GERALD FORD UNPACKED AT THE WHITE House. The Watergate cover-up trial began. Ford pardoned Richard Nixon. John Lennon released "Whatever Gets You Thru the Night."

I moved ninety-one miles down US 49 to enter Mississippi College, the Baptists' flagship school in the state since 1850. The clock tower of Nelson Hall rose over the oak-rimmed quadrangle's south edge, Provine Chapel to its east. The antebellum chapel with four looming stone columns had been General Ulysses S. Grant's Union hospital. "Truth and Virtue" was the Mississippi College motto. My parents delivered me to snug cherry-brick Hederman Hall—right behind Nelson's clock tower—as a freshman that August.

Four of us from Greenwood settled into the last two rooms at the end of Hederman's second floor. Ann and I, friends since third grade, were roommates. We made our beds with ribbed fire truck–red bedspreads from Sears and hung patchwork-print café curtains sewn by Ann's mother over the two windows. The yellow patches in the curtain print glowed when the sun hit the glass. The branches of a crepe myrtle tree swayed outside the windowpanes. All was sunny.

I was thrilled to be at MC—it was two hours beyond my tight Greenwood orbit and just outside of the state capital of Jackson. I lacked the social agility and sorority recommendations to be University of Mississippi material, and the idea of an out-of-state school horrified my parents—it could even possibly turn me into a Democrat, they sincerely worried. Mississippi College was my destiny. I was enrolling with the Baptists. I was one, of course, and the idea that we were all obligated to be nice to each other was a social plus to me. It was college with extraordinarily wide guardrails and a prim outer safety net.

That didn't mean my churchy self didn't want a guy. I might yellow-highlight *The Living Bible* passages that spoke to me in daily prayer time, but other times, I slapped the steering wheel to James Brown's "Get Up I Feel Like Being a Sex Machine" on the radio. Could I manage to be a player in college? I'd been transparent in high school—I don't mean full of candor; I mean invisible. I could go days in the Pillow Academy hallway without even talking to a boy. Dejected about that fact, I started a daily tally to see if I wasn't exaggerating the truth. No, I wasn't, the count reflected. Pretty much zero contact with guys every day.

To tell the truth, I was a little suspicious of my whole-hearted squeaky cleanliness myself. My morals had never been tested, since I'd never had an invitation to act otherwise. Not that I was gunning for having sex right away (against teachings and public propriety) or procuring a spouse—getting engaged in college was still common in Mississippi in the seventies and an indicator that you would indeed get to have sex eventually (right then, if quiet about it). I would be happy with simply an uptick in contact with guys. Any familiarity with a boy would be a step up.

The sun of the college social solar system was the Baptist Student Union. Being elected as the year's BSU president was as big a deal as being student body president or the quarterback on another campus. On arrival, one of the first events was the BSU project fair. I got the idea that BSU volunteering was as mandatory as freshman Biology. Postsupper one night in the student center's second-floor meeting room, our Greenwood quartet took our seats in the line of metal chairs to hear our options along with other freshmen.

"Welcome, y'all!" beamed a Tupelo sophomore with ear-length honey curls. She explained the after-school tutoring project at the nearby Baptist Children's Village. Then a jokey blond senior speech major from Laurel in plaid flare pants came up and declared, "Things you can't say, puppets can!" In his right hand was a yarn-headed lady puppet. His hand was up her rear. He shared that he and a half-dozen others chauffeured their puppets to church suppers and youth groups within the BSU van's driving range on Sunday nights. An earnest, smileless, lanky education major spoke next to recruit afternoon visitors to the Mississippi Crippled Children's Hospital. Despite the draw of March of Dimes in Greenwood, I didn't jump at the chance to be on her crew at the awfully named facility.

A warm-eyed, busty junior with a peanut-brown pageboy talked up the Hour of Power Choir. Ann and our two other Greenwood dormmates, Wanda and Sandra, sat up. HOP Choir, for short, was branded as more fun than the music department's hard-core choir for voice majors requiring auditions, Handel, and severe black concert dresses. HOP Choir singers wore pine-green maxidresses in a white flower-sprig print and winged their program of hymns. They toured the same kind of nearby churches as the puppet posse on Sunday nights in a BSU vehicle. Fun maxidress or not, I passed. The idea somehow didn't hit me.

Next up was the Helping Hand Rescue Mission. Project chair Palmer Carr had a male model's square jaw, sweet blue eyes, and wavy praline-brown hair thick enough to be in a TRESemmé conditioner ad.

"Everybody can use a friend and a listening ear. That's what we do," Palmer Carr explained. There was something oddly mature, craggy, and masculine about Palmer's face. It was the reverse of how some men stay baby faced into middle age. In retrospect, the electricity flashing inside my mind over Palmer Carr's pitch indicated my subconscious was up to something. If I couldn't have a boyfriend, I could at least edge in the direction of free-floating masculinity and adjacency. I had nothing to lose.

At Helping Hand, BSU members led a chapel service and stayed to talk until the men's 6 p.m. supper. "We care that they're there," Palmer said. He talked about connecting with shelter guys as they were, not as a maneuver aimed to try to convert them. I liked that. Anyway, befriending a person first struck me as a ground floor requirement before selling them on our version of salvation. From my second-row chair, I drank in Palmer's words. I was beyond thirsty.

Helping Hand, founded by white Jackson Baptist men in 1961, ran on the classic strings-attached Salvation Army rescue mission model created in Victorian Britain. The operation offered homeless men the four Ss: soup, sleep, soap, and salvation. If a man agreed to listen to the spiritual pitch, the mission offered the other three Ss for the night. There have been worse deals.

The next Tuesday at 5 p.m. I met the other volunteers at the BSU van. Besides Palmer, there were seven or so others. I folded into the back as we hummed toward Jackson. Randy, a church-music major, brought his guitar, which poked into the cloth ceiling ahead of me. He shared the middle seat with Milton, a Louisiana ministerial student with a pale face, dark Beatle haircut, and a leather jacket. Pine trees flowed by on I-20. A few minutes later we passed the outskirts of southwest Jackson. We pulled up to a white concrete block building at 426 West Silas Brown, close enough to Capitol Street, the city's modest urban heart, that the cluster of tall downtown office buildings poked up on the north horizon.

Inside the mission's glass double doors in the common room, a few lodgers expressionlessly eyed us on arrival.

"Hello there." A slight man with slicked-down black hair and an unplaceable accent stepped over. "Good to have you back." He had a slate-blue worker's shirt on and an air of being in charge. His gray skin morphed dark purple under his weary-looking eyes. The smells of musky clothes and supper frying nearby floated in the air. The wood-paneled walls held handwritten signs: NO PROFANITY and NO FIGHTING and NO DAY LOITERING BEFORE 5 P.M. CHECK-IN. The men's faces didn't look as if they'd been waiting for the pleasure of having college Baptists arrive to cheer their day. A number strategically looked down at the worn wood floor rather than at us.

Meanwhile, the right side of the room was prepped for the service.

"Okay, we sit down now," the guy in the work shirt directed the lodgers, whose dress was heavy on dirty flannel, worn-out sweatshirts, smudged ball caps, and greasy hair. The men ambled to the chairs, which croaked with scraping noises on the floor as everyone sat. At the front of the chair rows was a white-painted wooden pulpit, its front decorated with a black outline of a cross and Jesus Saves in Old English letters.

Worn copies of the Baptist hymnal rested on each seat. I took a chair in the middle with a clear view of the pulpit, the better to admire Palmer. The people in our posse who were part of the service filled the first row.

To start things off, Palmer scanned the gathering, his blue eyes gifting us—well, gifting me. An extra whoosh of oxygen filled my lungs. "Glad to see everyone tonight," he said. "Let's begin with prayer."

The head Helping Hand guy in the blue work shirt—Zeke, I learned—stood in the back. No lodger looked delighted over the service, but none looked hostile either. Whatever was on their minds—the upcoming supper, likely—they knew the rules and played by them, at least looking as if they were paying attention.

"Our Heavenly Father, we thank you for this opportunity to be together," Palmer began.

Everyone bowed their heads, in respect to God and probably of Zeke since he was the flesh-and-blood enforcer. Given a 2020s read of service participation, the conduct code was off back then. Service participation was defined as respectfully not uttering a peep unless time to sing.

"Bless us all as we worship you. In Jesus's name, amen." As eyelids lifted, Palmer gave a nod to Randy, who shot up from the first row with his guitar.

"Let's sing 'Amazing Grace.'" Randy's fingers found their position. "Page 330 if you'd like to see the words." He strummed and sang:

Amazing grace! how sweet the sound, That saved a wretch like me!

Self-image-wise, the wretch part was kind of harsh, a little too close to home for our crowd. Some of the lodgers sang along under the blink-less watch of Zeke. Others just eyed our song leader with blank-faced endurance. Then there was the always-popular choice among some of the lodgers to keep their focus on the well-examined wood floor and their janky tennis shoes.

I flipped to page 330 after the first verse.

When we've been there ten thousand years, Bright shining as the sun,
We've no less days to sing God's praise Than when we first begun.

That line about the inconsequence of ten millennia in God's eyes still always catches my attention. Back at age eighteen, though, the words on the cosmic concept of time hit me particularly hard as well, since time creeped in my case. I was out of high school and into college yet still on the sidelines. Would time ever produce more than the predictable for me?

College freshmen who arrived ill prepared for English got a remedial course. I needed the social equivalent. My awkwardness knotted me around others, guys most of all. My brain froze and, with it, any ability at open-air conversation. The boy-shaped hole inside me throughout high school accompanied me to campus. Should I have cared so much for guy validation? Of course not. But a big part of me hungered for it in order to regard myself as a full, legitimate member the human family. And why wouldn't I want to experience what I longed to, anyway?

"Amazing Grace" finished, Randy vacated the pulpit and resumed his seat. Palmer moved back behind the pulpit, his fingers resting self-consciously on each side of its top. He cast those baby blues over the crowd. "Let's think a little about God's care." Palmer's head tilted, silence between his sentences. "The words of 'Amazing Grace' sink in deep, don't they?"

To my inner approval, Palmer presented one mild side of an unassuming conversation instead of a scorcher of a sermon. A ministerial student, Palmer packed kindness instead of an eye for sizing up the guys as potential notches on his salvation score card.

"God's arms are open to us all, no matter if we're here in this room or out in Jackson or back at Mississippi College," he noted.

I made out the smell of hamburger meat frying and maybe hot, steamy canned corn coming from the kitchen.

Palmer continued, "Through the good times and the bad ones. God's arms have sure been open to me when I've made mistakes. And I've made more than my share." Palmer's square jawline looked just as good in Helping Hand's scanty incandescent light as it had in the student union. He scanned everyone seated. He paused, easy with the quiet.

"I guess what I want to say," he said, "is that I hope things work out for you. All of us visiting here tonight do. So does God." Palmer turned his face. "Randy, I bet you have another song before these good folks go to supper."

Randy stepped back to the front. "How about 'What a Friend We Have in Jesus'?" He thwacked the first chords.

Jesus knows our ev'ry weakness, Take it to the Lord in prayer.

"Milton, will you lead us in the benediction?" Palmer asked when the hymn was over.

Milton, the long-haired, leather-jacketed senior from Louisiana did just that. Chair legs squealed when everyone stood up. Finally time for my part: conversation with the lodgers. For my first chat, a lodger standing by himself would be easiest. None were, though. A number clumped close to the kitchen door. Some talked low, and others carefully looked down, hoping to be left alone. If they could run out the clock, we'd depart and supper would begin. Two noticed that I was looking in their direction and instantly turned their backs. The body language was all it took for me to give up on conversation. So much for care on my part. As staff, Zeke was getting paid to tolerate us. I'd try him since he couldn't turn his back. He stood in the center of the room, his eyes still sweeping everyone. Clatter continued inside the kitchen.

I tried him. "Hi. I'm Ellen Ann."

Below his sad-dog, dark-bagged eyes, a courteous smile flickered for a moment. "I'm Zeke."

"Nice to meet you, Zeke."

Silence.

"I'm from Greenwood. Where are you from, Zeke?"

"Detroit. I lived in Detroit." He sighed. "I was an electrician. I came home one day, and they'd left me. My wife. My three children. Gone."

"Oh no." I shook my head.

"They took everything, my family. I've not heard from them anymore." Zeke's accent wasn't Midwestern, maybe Eastern European. His intonations were a mystery for another day, though. "I stayed in our place. I waited. No word ever. So I left. Quit work. Headed out. Ended up here." He looked at me while he talked and then remembered to watch the men. His eyes shot around the room. He turned back to me, furrowing the bridge of his nose. "No one bothered you, did they?" His forehead creased. "They're not supposed to bother you."

"Oh no. We came to talk. We want to visit everyone."

"They're not supposed to ask you for money, either," he continued. "No one asked you for any money, did they?"

"No."

Thankfully, our time was done. Palmer was at the front door. "Thank y'all for letting us visit." This was tantamount to Let's Eat for lodgers who knew the nightly drill. "We'll see you next week, Zeke."

"See you Tuesday," I said.

Zeke waved sadly at Palmer. He nodded somberly my way, too, before looking at the men, gesturing toward the kitchen doorway. "Okay. Now. Get in line."

Everyone queued at the entry to the kitchen.

Back in the van, I listened to the others critique their parts in the service. In the back row of the vehicle as we rumbled back to campus, I mulled Palmer. I could see his outline against the front windshield. His unassuming touch with the lodgers made me melt even more. If I was auditioning Helping Hand Tuesdays, it had met my expectations, admittedly vague as they were, even to me. Before long, the van purred into its regular parking spot on campus. We climbed out.

"So, what did you think?" Palmer asked.

"It was great," I said as brilliant comeback.

"See you next week."

I planned on it.

Next Tuesday, our van left campus on precise schedule. Milton drove via I-20 with the same volunteers as before plus a piano-playing friend of Randy's.

"We need to mix more with the fellas this time," Palmer said in the front. "We don't need to stay to ourselves."

"It's hard getting them to talk," said Randy.

I nodded for both truths.

Milton led the service. Randy led reruns of last week's "Amazing Grace" and "What a Friend We Have in Jesus." His friend slipped into position at the blond-wood piano with a tone as flat as you'd expect. Eventually, Palmer closed with the benediction. Chairs groaned as everyone stood up. The impending supper featured lots of onions, if smell was an indicator.

This Tuesday's overnighters utilized the same eye avoidance as last week's. A few more turned their back when I looked primed to come over and talk. Despite unenthusiastic body language, I approached a trio of men staring at their dusty shoes.

"Hello. I'm Ellen Ann."

The first guy had deep trenches in his russet sunburned cheeks. Dirty hair strands curled at the collar of his faded cobalt plaid shirt. "Hi."

Pleased with the triumph of squeezing a syllable out of my very first lodger, I pressed on. "What's your name?"

"Ed." Nothing further. One and done, it looked like. Maybe the other two would talk to me.

"I'm Ellen Ann. What's your name?"

"JT." He had a froth of peroxided hair and eyes glued to his laceless worker boots.

"What's yours?" I asked the third guy.

"Ireshush."

"I'm sorry. What did you say?"

"Ireshush."

Ireshush wasn't his name, but that was the best I made out. He had stubble, a hunting cap, and a smoker's acrid smell. "Got any cigarettes?" he asked.

"No."

Silence. His eyes dropped to the floor.

In my peripheral vision, I noted Palmer alongside a guy in a tent of an army jacket. "How're you tonight, sir?"

"Good." Palmer didn't extract any more surplus syllables than I, which soothed my sense of Helping Hand inadequacy. Yet making BSU friends wasn't on the army-jacket guy's hierarchy of needs, nor Ireshush's, nor any of these guys' lists, it was clear.

I'd met my failure quota for the night. Back to Zeke, keeping tabs, of course, from the center of the room. His eyes swabbed the room, checking the lodgers.

"Hi, Zeke. I'm Ellen Ann. We talked last week."

He nodded without smiling. He cast his eyes over my shoulder to squint at the men. Then his eyes came back to me. No sign of recognition.

"You're okay, aren't you?" His tone sounded as if he doubted it. "No one's bothering you, are they?"

"No. We came here to talk."

He shook his head. "No one is supposed to bother you." His slate-blue worker's shirt had ZEKE stitched in script over the pocket, I noticed this time. "You have to be careful."

I smiled. "No one here says much, do they?"

Zeke ignored the question and answered one I didn't ask. "I came here from Detroit. I was an electrician. I came home from work one day, and my wife and children were gone." He shook his head with a weary look. "They took everything. They never called again. After a while I left. Ended up here."

It was the same story as the week before. Maybe with the nightly turnover in lodgers, Zeke only needed one basic topic of conversation. He had fairly new sets of ears every evening, while repeat lodgers knew going along with Zeke was the price of one more nightly supper and a bed.

Our drill repeated every Tuesday. The BSU van at five. Arrival at the mission at five twenty. First a twenty-minute service, then twenty minutes of trying to pry conversation out of close-mouthed lodgers. Boxes checked off, the lodgers then got to head to the supper line while we chugged back to campus until the next Tuesday.

I'd learned more about Helping Hand by this point. The Helping Hand board had high hopes that the shelter would serve as a muscular conversion program. Our BSU delegation was merely one evening's slot in a nightly rotation of groups expected to win lodger souls with sermon, song, and reminders of sin. Our postservice conversation was supposed to help seal the salvation deal with men whose ears had either been scared or softened by the sermon. Over the first weeks, it was clear the lodgers weren't especially hungry for our smiling college selves with clean clothes and lives. They were hungry, unsurprisingly, for the supper.

Tuesday by Tuesday, two more things became obvious. First there was a hitch in the salvation campaign in that Palmer's sermons weren't the brimstone type. The second blockage's name was Zeke. Contrary to Helping Hand's goals, Zeke was determined to discourage contact between us and the boarders, salvation at stake or not. Zeke believed in preventing potential tension before it started. Later in life I got that. As a Brandon High French teacher in charge of keeping order in a restless room of thirty, I later took the same approach as Zeke: do yourself a favor and cut idle conversation out so trouble has no chance to start.

On Zeke's watch, he boiled down his boarder expectations to three things: listen to the service, don't ask volunteer visitors like us for money, and, no matter our eagerness, keep a distance during our meet and greet. When your cot and 6 p.m. plate of canned beans and macaroni are on the line, why would the men defy him? Homelessness is full of navigation all day, every day; we BSUers were easy step arounds.

Here's something also obvious to everyone in the BSU van, including Palmer: my crush on him. I was embarrassed at its obviousness, but my sighs and helpless goo-goo eyes paid off. Palmer asked me to homecoming in October. My mind ran wild. Were we destined for each other? Maybe we'd run a rescue mission of our own someday, Zeke-less and therefore free to flow with easy connection. For extra points, our rescue mission would up the geographic ante; its location might be an African capital or an Indian city. At least a distance from I-20 and local baseline social expectations that I couldn't wrangle.

On homecoming night, Palmer picked me up in the Hederman dorm lobby. "Well, you look nice," he said with his customary kindness. I was in a pair of pool-green palazzo pants and a peplum top that I'd bought three days before at JCPenney. I wore flat sandals (with gray knee socks, inexplicably) to keep from being taller than he.

I had Palmer to myself. My skull throbbed with that thrill. "Thank you," I said, a sparkly, witty reply that was predictive of the whole night to come, unfortunately.

At Poet's, a Jackson fern bar, I tried to hold up my end of the conversation over shrimp remoulade. "What are you going to do after May?"

"Maybe seminary. Maybe just go back to Winona and get a job for a while," he said over his cheeseburger. "I have two great-aunts who're like grandmothers to me. It'd be nice to spend a little time with them," he said. "Seminary'll be there in another year. I can save money too." He took a sip of his drink, then picked his cheeseburger back up. "You're a French major? Tough subject." He shook his head. "Greek came close to killing me." On campus, the two-year slog through Greek was a miserable rite for ministerial students—not the kind of Greek that's helpful on a Carnival cruise stop on Mykonos, but the archaic New Testament kind, handy in the Roman Empire.

As I crunched lettuce, I made sure to keep my pressed lips in a pleasant smile. He was as nice as always. I was awkward as always. The conversation was . . . nice.

Even at the early stage of the night, even with my lack of social radar, my insides said that the two of us didn't have much to talk about. The electricity inside me started to ebb as we struggled for conversation. There would be no we and no future rescue shelter, not abroad, not alongside I-20, not anywhere. At the end of the night, Palmer pecked me on the cheek at the Hederman entryway. "See you Tuesday," he said.

The next Tuesday, Palmer's customary kindheartedness—and nothing more—signaled a truth. It had been as Palmeresque to ask me to homecoming as it was for him to visit Helping Hand. I had been as needy in terms of his good-deed checklist as the Helping Hand guys. He never asked me out again, nor did his sweet, benevolent smile ever change either. A few times as the year moved on, I spotted him leaving on a date with a senior named Sharon who lived in Gunter Hall, an upperclassman dorm next to mine. Arm in arm, the pair leaned into each other, talking and laughing as they went. I sighed. Such is life. Such is the missed boat.

I kept going to Helping Hand. So did Palmer and Milton until they graduated. I never improved at conversations or conversions. Zeke remained Zeke. If the Helping Hand board monitored the Christian conversion count, it looked to be approximately zero. But I can't say our sessions did any harm.

What I do know is that Helping Hand helped me. Tuesday night at Helping Hand was just my kind of remedial class as a freshman. Not everyone goes to a homeless shelter to meet guys, but I did. I look back and see how I picked that completely male project as the closest thing I could find to a male intro class for myself. As good instruction typically is, the teaching was multiapproach. I practiced nudging myself into icebreaker conversation with reluctant lodgers. The weekly Zeke exchange resembled a guided conversation in a beginner French textbook in which students repeat set lines until the awkward becomes smoothly automatic. In the BSU van, there was chatter with Palmer, Milton, Randy, and the occasional other aspiring preacher. Confidence grows in increments and petite triumphs in beginner lessons from sexuality to paddleboarding.

Due to the backward fact that Baptists forbid female clergy, the other Helping Hand volunteers test-driving their preministerial chops were resultingly male only. No matter the unfairness of the pulpit sexism that caused it, if I wanted default-male immersion, I had run across a high-concentration scenario, a total fit.

John Lennon's "Whatever Gets You Thru the Night" was not only on the radio that year but in the air. It's a well-loved song and well-worn truth. We make our way through what's possible, even as we dream and angle for more to come.

It took a year of college to get my footing. The next August our Greenwood quartet moved to the third floor of upperclassman Latimer-Webb dorm. Ann and I switched from the primary brights of our Hederman room to what we saw as befittingly sophomore and more sophisticated: bamboo window shades and new Sears bedspreads in earth brown this time. We had the requisite macramé hanging planters too.

My confidence and sense of self grew month by month. By March, I finally managed to have sex. On that milestone Friday evening, habitual rule follower that I was, I was back at the dorm from my boyfriend's rental house two blocks from campus in ample time for the women's midnight curfew. I rationalized premarital sex to my nervous conscience by telling myself I would marry the guy eventually. We did date a few months. When I recently Googled him, I saw he was disbarred not long ago. Here's something else interesting and maybe coincidental of that time and place, but maybe not: The MC president from my era pleaded guilty in 1996 to mail fraud, tax evasion, and money laundering. He was sentenced to seven years in prison for stealing $2.8 million from the college through an intricate web of bank accounts, accused of using donation money to bankroll prostitutes, luxury gifts, and personal brokerage accounts. Interestingly, same as the Helping Hand guys, I remember the president's furtive eyes and his skittishness at meeting the gaze of others in conversation.

The John Lennon mantra is a solid truth in a shelter, on a campus, inside the college president's suite, or in the BSU. While we live inside systems, we can work with what we've got that very day at that very moment to tide us over until we get to the next way station.

I've checked recently to see what I can find out about Helping Hand. Near downtown Jackson, the building is empty with a Christ Churches International, Inc. sign over the locked, familiar glass double doors. Searching online turned up twelve stories in the *Jackson Clarion-Ledger* over time, starting with an article on the mission's 1961 founding until its last mention in 1985. The final article reported Helping Hand was adding a wing for women. There's no further mention of the mission after that, nor any record of it at all in the archives of the Mississippi Baptist Convention, MC, the MC Baptist Student Union, or with anyone I've asked.

My memory keeps its own records, though. On those Tuesday nights my freshman year, all the guys—the lodgers, Zeke, Palmer, Milton, and the occasional other hopeful preacher in the BSU van— earnestly and generously gave a helping hand to me.

Chapter 10

Private Household Occupations

HOUSEMAIDS PREDATE HOUSES. EVEN ON A GOOD DAY, THE physical and psychic proximity of a maid to the family she works for turns into enmeshment. In the book of Genesis, Sarah and her maid Hagar made each other mutually miserable in a desert tent camp. Four thousand years later, the quarter-century marriage of Arnold Schwarzenegger and Maria Shriver fell apart because their maid got pregnant on the job, as did Hagar all those years before. Prostitution is said to be the world's oldest profession, but I have to believe domestic work is the likelier winner of the title.

Poor Black women, the near-universal housemaid labor force in the post–Civil War South, have been idealized—and collectivized—in fiction and in film by characters like the saintly Calpurnia of *To Kill a Mockingbird* or Aibileen of *The Help*. The Black maids of the American South were cast as an "irrefutable collective verity," to borrow the term that Edward W. Said, author of *Orientalism*, used for the way humans lump others into hazy yet impermeable generalizations. In southern history, to talk about a housemaid was to talk about the strictures of race and gender that prevented most Black women from finding a better job.

Where I live, in Jackson, Mississippi, the prototypical Black household maid still in the workforce today is likely a woman fifty-five or older who started working for a family twenty or more years ago. The not-so-young housemaid works for an equally not-so-young customer—someone like me. At fifty-seven, I dated back to before the civil rights era. My hometown of Greenwood was on the movement map, the suspected inspiration for the Bob Dylan song

"Maggie's Farm." (Dylan stopped at the nearby Magee family farm for a rally in 1963.) I was seven in 1963, old enough to notice the change in tone of adult conversations and to comprehend snippets from network correspondents in recognizable towns as I flipped channels on the den RCA. Our 1955 black-and-white TV was on its last legs in 1963, as was the society outside the den's fiberglass café curtains. Within a year, my parents replaced the old set with a sleek walnut-veneer Admiral color model. The stamp of history inside human heads is not updated as easily.

• • •

Mrs. Mable Sanders began working in my house in 1991, at age fifty, to earn extra money after her husband's death. She'd arrive on Tuesdays, and I'd hand over my diapered daughter—my older daughter was already in kindergarten—and bolt out the door faster than you could say "Thai House lunch special." Tuesday was my morning to run errands, volunteer at a Junior League daycare project, and meet a friend for *panang* curry chicken before returning home to pay Mrs. Sanders and reclaim my offspring.

Once my younger daughter started preschool, Mrs. Sanders kept coming to do the chores I didn't want to do. Around noon, I'd hear her let herself in the front door with her key. The wash cycle would thump on in the laundry room down the hall, and the clank of dishes sounded from the kitchen along with the exhale of running water. Six feet tall with broad cheeks, Mrs. Sanders swept, mopped, and made beds as I came and went from the house all afternoon. She wore a sweatshirt and knit cotton jogging pants. She added a navy knit cap sometimes, while other days her short gray hair was crimped in precise pin waves around her head. Her gaze was always congenial behind her pink opaline-framed glasses. We exchanged aimless chitchat, often about life with school-age children since the two granddaughters who lived with her were nearly the same age as Kate and Molly. Sometimes we talked about racial injustice—in general terms of local and national politics—and she told stories of navigating Jim Crow life in 1940s-era Copiah County and Jackson in the 1960s.

Time moved along. My girls departed for college, and so did Mrs. Sanders's two granddaughters. After I had employed her for nearly twenty years, our arrangement changed; I started swapping Tuesday cleanups with my now ex-husband, who wanted Mrs. Sanders's help at his new residence. One afternoon a few years ago, Mrs. Sanders, slowing down with arthritis and hitting age seventy, lost her balance while sweeping his living room. She fell on the pinewood floor, struggled to get up, and decided it was time to retire. That brings us to the present. Every few months, I bring Mrs. Sanders—now seventy-four, on Social Security, and homebound with both arthritis and diabetes—a half-dozen bottles of insulin, courtesy of a doctor friend who sets aside pharmaceutical freebies. The doctor knows Mrs. Sanders because she did housework for his family in 1963, when he was eight. Jackson is a pretty small pond.

Now that I have decided to parse my relationship with Mrs. Sanders, I am nervous as I try to portray myself as sensitive in the way that whites—earnest middle-aged Mississippians like me, anyway—do when they're in racially touchy territory. My employment of Mrs. Sanders puts me in some quasi–book of Judgment, the post–civil rights movement Mississippi section that exists in my head and in that of Mrs. Sanders—even now, our matching Obama bumper stickers faded and peeling.

Jackson is a Black-majority town led by Black mayors and police chiefs for many administrations. Yet in the microcosm of my ranch house as Mrs. Sanders and I made small talk, I often felt us sliding into mutual representatives of history. We were both aware of what the other represented in a way that people born after 1975, and maybe non-Mississippians, simply aren't. Race was the very subtext of our relationship.

• • •

My tie to Mrs. Sanders brings up two unsettling points. For southern-ers our age, the weight of history still presses on seemingly benign Black-white relationships. Generations have perceptions based on what signature events marked that population's formative years. Collective generational memory is the term for how perceptions are formed by events that happened in our lives from childhood up to age thirty, the theory goes. For our skulls with the Mississippi time stamp, Mrs. Sanders and I can't sidestep the memories we pack.

My second point dates back to long before civil rights and the Civil War. The book of Genesis is only twelve chapters past the Garden of Eden when it presents evidence that humans, given an extra bit of clout, are apt to lord it over others. Sarah banished Hagar because she could. Jacob stepped on his brother Esau given the opportunity. Likewise, I had the upper hand in our deal, and I had no intention of relinquishing it. That unsavory impulse is nothing new. I was no trailblazer, nor was one of Mrs. Sanders's other customers who plays a major role in our story. We'll call her Barbara.

During Mrs. Sanders's workweek, I was one of a half-dozen cus-tomers on her schedule. So was Barbara. Out in public—I knew the woman casually—Barbara was an energetic octogenarian with a friendly manner and twinkle in her eyes. As a woman, she had herself navigated a restricted sea of opportunity. The ever-smiling Barbara had channeled her talent and public pep into heading the town's Junior League for a term. (Jackson is the kind of place where the accomplishment of being an ex–Junior League president stays with you for the rest of your life, like playing SEC football or being in the Peace Corps.) "We need to send the Blacks back to Africa" is typical of what Barbara would say, somehow obtuse to her offen-siveness. Behind her back, Mrs. Sanders mimicked Barbara in a prissy, clipped white-talk imitation that swished with ridiculous self-importance. Mrs. Sanders called Barbara out on the Africa dec-laration, leading Barbara to add, "Well, the criminal Blacks, I mean."

Over the years, Mrs. Sanders reported a running catalog of Bar-bara's outrages. The woman routinely forgot to leave Mrs. Sanders's pay for weeks on end. One freezing Christmas Eve, Mrs. Sanders was supposed to depart to attend her own family's Christmas party while Barbara's holiday dinner was still in progress. Barbara had been irritated when Mrs. Sanders warned her that she would only work up until 6 p.m. At six, Mrs. Sanders couldn't find her coat. She ended up staying longer to look for it and, unsurprisingly, inevitably also ended up continuing to help Barbara shuttle dishes for her dinner underway. As Barbara's dinner wound down, Mrs. Sanders found her coat—mysteriously stuffed in Barbara's trash can outside. Mrs. Sanders was positive Barbara did it to keep her at the house.

Looking back, I realize that the Barbara anecdotes were more than just gallows humor from the Barbara wars. Mrs. Sanders turned Barbara's gall into a kind of indirect language to reiterate to me unacceptable job behavior. The impulse to use indirect language, of course, indicated the limit to our own candor—a line I wish I could say hadn't existed. True, our conversations about race and our offspring in general were easy. But talking about politics, decades-past memories, and offspring was one thing. Talking about us two specifically was a different matter. We never talked about her pay.

I didn't ask Mrs. Sanders what she wanted to be paid, and she never said. I had no idea what her other customers paid her, but I left her a flat forty dollars for the cleanup, which would have come to about nine or ten dollars an hour. Mrs. Sanders never asked for more, and I never officially gave her a raise, though I rationalized that omission by adding another ten- or twenty-dollar bill from time to time and paying for the Tuesdays when I was out of town. (I also got her a raise for her gig with my ex by telling him that her charge was sixty dollars, not the forty that, in truth, I paid her myself.) But try as I did to justify the arrangement, the fact is I didn't increase Mrs. Sanders's pay outright for more than fifteen years. The extras were tips—grand discretionary gestures that meant she had to thank me when I did give her more than forty dollars. That I remember all the details and justifications of paying her proves that I felt uneasy about the arrangement, even then. Would I have paid a white house cleaner more? Maybe not, but with a commercial cleaning service, there would have been an outright conversation about the fee.

In her fine oral history, *Telling Memories Among Southern Women: Domestic Workers and Their Employers in the Segregated South*, Susan Tucker notes how in the Jim Crow era, white female employers augmented their Black domestics' minimal pay with left-over food and used household goods. The practice became a ritual-ized part of the relationship, an echo of the nineteenth-century "ser-vice pan," or the dish that a domestic worker in a southern kitchen used to carry leftovers home. An entire chapter of Tucker's history, "Giving and Receiving," examines the common act of supplementing a worker's low pay with "gifts"—food or cast-off household items—and the accompanying assumption that the worker was supposed to be grateful. The offerings permitted the employer to come across as thoughtful, yet also shored up her sense of her own superiority.

• • •

A logical date to mark the start of wider employment opportuni-ties for Black women in Jackson would be the enactment of the Civil Rights Act, on July 2, 1964. The historic legislation outlawed discrimination based on race, color, religion, or national origin. When the act went into effect, the local daily *Clarion-Ledger* printed a front-page news story that included an off-handed disclaimer about discriminatory classified advertising under the law: "This could lead to changes in the traditional 'help wanted, men' and 'help wanted, women' ads in newspapers," although the advertiser, not the newspaper, would be held responsible for breaking the law, the story claimed. Yet as before, thirty-nine pages over, the *Clarion-Ledger* continued, as always, to run advertisements for positions such as: "WHITE assistant manager for McLemore's Texaco Service Station," "WHITE waitress, experience not necessary, age 18–25," "COLORED cook, experienced, for residence, 2 until 9 p.m."

Even so, a shift was occurring in Jackson. Another milestone in wider opportunity was a February 1965 hearing conducted in Jackson by the US Commission on Civil Rights. Longtime Missis-sippi journalist Bill Minor covered the multiday hearing for the *New*

Orleans Times-Picayune and recalled how the event brought out the first rational response by the local white establishment. "Moderation had reared its head in Mississippi," wrote *New York Times* reporter Roy Reed about the tenor of the session. Police harassment persisted along with impediments to voter registration, but finally there was testimony from influential white figures calling for the end of violent resistance to equal rights. Reed's account noted that in addition to fact-finding, the hearing had an "implied purpose—to work on the conscience of white Mississippi." Minor remembered how after the hearing, major businesses in Jackson started hiring Black employees for conspicuous jobs. Black assistant managers and bank tellers became a part of the Capitol Street workforce, along with another sight Minor hadn't seen before: Black and white coworkers eating lunch together downtown.

The Help, the best-selling novel by Kathryn Stockett, a Jackson native, follows an interconnected cast of Jackson maids and housewives during the early 1960s. Two occurrences make up the end: the fall from power of Hilly Holbrook, a white supremacist, socialite bully, and the publication of a tell-all book about the working lives of a dozen Jackson maids, secretly cocreated by Skeeter Phelan, an outlier Junior Leaguer, and Aibileen Clark, a longtime maid who serves as the novel's heart.

For the filming of the Tate Taylor adaptation, dozens of northeast Jackson women gamely set aside their customary Ann Taylor and Tory Burch appetite to enter a time warp back fifty years as shirt-waisted, high-haired extras. Predictably, many people from northeast Jackson—the *Clarion-Ledger*'s once routine phrase "fashionable northeast Jackson" describes both a map location and a mindset—also put energy into speculating over the real local identity of every character. Not everyone was amused by the story, though, including Grace Sweet, eighty-two. Mrs. Sweet stands apart from the other Jackson women who felt burned by Stockett's portrait of employers of household help; she actually issued a book in response. Mrs. Sweet also happens to be Black.

I had tea with Mrs. Sweet at her two-story townhome in northeast Jackson to discuss *The Help* and her response to it. In her living room, Victorian-era family furniture surrounded us, as well as framed family mementoes like her husband's four-foot lace-scalloped christening gown from 1905, hanging in a shadow box over the mantle. Photos of family members with Bill Clinton, Sargent Shriver, and President Obama hung on the walls.

Mrs. Sweet took issue with how *The Help* reduced Jackson to well-off whites and low-income Blacks. "It just pictured all white women as rich and having maids, and all Black women as maids," she said. "Not every Black woman worked in somebody's kitchen." Mrs. Sweet, a biology teacher and guidance counselor in Jackson Public Schools for thirty years, doesn't dispute that Black maids were mistreated in the city. Her complaint is that the book gave the impression that all Black women in Jackson worked as domestics.

The Sweet family is prominent. Mrs. Sweet's daughter Denise Sweet Owens has remained on the bench as a chancery judge in Jackson for thirty-three years. Her son, Dennis, is one of Mississippi's most high-profile trial attorneys. Younger daughter Selika is a family practice physician. Mrs. Sweet's extended family includes a PhD and eight more medical doctors. Born two years after the Civil War, Mrs. Sweet's father graduated from college in Indiana before returning to Mississippi as a Methodist minister.

Mrs. Sweet earned her master's degree in biology from Baton Rouge's Southern University in the early 1960s, a time when graduate programs at Mississippi's white universities weren't open to her. Published in 2013 by the History Press and coauthored by Benjamin Bradley, Sweet's book *Church Street: The Sugar Hill of Jackson, Mississippi* is a history of the professional Black community that existed in Jackson in the first half of the twentieth century. The title is a reference to the affluent Harlem neighborhood of Sugar Hill, nicknamed for the comfortable, sweet life in the enclave from 145th to 155th Streets. In Mrs. Sweet's childhood, Church Street was home to Jackson's African American professionals. She lived across the street from a physician's family who employed a full-time maid, gardener, and chauffeur. This same resident owned three hundred rental houses.

When she worked, Mrs. Sweet employed full-time help from 1953 until 1969, and it took one-third of her salary to pay her housekeeper appropriately. "I treated them as professionals," she said. Her maid wore regular clothes instead of a white uniform, was addressed as "Mrs.," and was included as a guest on family occasions. One housekeeper of Mrs. Sweet's quit to take a better-paying job with a white family. She returned to the Sweet household the next day, however, after her new employer asked her to crawl under the house and pull out the dog.

The book version of *The Help* has sold more than ten million copies, and the film adaptation has generated more than $200 million in worldwide revenue. Despite and because of its success, the story has become a lightning rod. The Association of Black Women Historians notes that by omitting Klan violence, civil rights activism by Blacks, and the issue of sexual assault on Black housemaids, Stockett's portrayal of the era is distorted.

My leeriness reared up on the first page, at the sight of the phonetically written passages of Black dialect. It was unsettling to see— and therefore be conscious of—the editorial choice to print the maids' voices in dialect. It seemed as though the snippy housewives of the novel weren't the only ones diminishing the maids' dignity; the book I was holding did, too. All southerners know the layers of assumptions tied to the sound of an accent. Unfairly, I think, none of the white charactahs' nonstandard pronunciation is spahtlighted by funny spellin'. Initially I found it hard to focus on the content of what the dialect-speaking characters had to say. Once I settled in, however, my attention shifted to the humor of the ironic, dry lip service that the maids marshaled as they went about placating their employers. A frequent criticism of *The Help* is the patronizing quality of its white-girl-to-the-rescue plot. Stockett makes patronization a two-way business, though. The reader witnesses the maids' silent exasperation and righteous anger, but we're also privy to the blistering satire that comes through the maids' show of fake servitude to the white world during work hours. (Mrs. Sanders got a kick out of the film, particularly when the maid Minny Jackson feeds the villain Hilly excrement-laced pie—talk about a recipe that is truly signature.) Being a maid is "a real Fourth of July picnic," Minny vents to Aibileen. "It's what we dream a doing all weekend, get back in they houses to polish they silver." She continues, "We love they kids when they little. . . . And then they turn out just like they mamas."

The double standard dialect issue evaporates in the film and audio versions of *The Help*. Alice Walker recommends the audio form. "When I began listening to *The Help*, I found myself seeing my mother's sacrifice and love at an even greater depth than I had before. . . . I finished the novel, late in the night, and after many tears and some laughter," she wrote on her blog. Walker lived in Jackson from 1967 until 1971, when she was married to NAACP attorney Mel Leventhal. On her blog, she noted that she had initial misgivings on hearing about the novel, but she had no criticism of what Stockett included and omitted in the domestic, female-centered story. "This is why fiction exists," she wrote. "To tell the story in the only way you can, given the reality of one's limitations."

I once heard a frustrated fiction writer give a sarcastic prescription for commercial creative success: treat a horrific subject in a way that lets the audience feel relief. Taking on racial injustice gets a hopeful ending in *The Help*. Hilly Holbrook is an easy-to-hate cutout whose cartoonish cruelty frees readers from any self-examination of their own potential for complicity in racially unjust systems. No one can possibly identify with Stockett's Mean Girl (her nonhuman, alien delight in eating excrement is as psychologically ham-handed as it comes). And *The Help*'s saintly maid Aibileen Clark is equally unchallenging, a nurturing and maternal Black woman with an inherently loving disposition. Like Harper Lee's Calpurnia, William Faulkner's Dilsey, and Margaret Mitchell's Mammy, Stockett's Aibileen trades on our devotion and unconditional love for the archetypal mother figure. Aibileen has made a career of raising

seventeen white children, beginning in 1924. Further, her greatest
wound comes from her own experience as a mother: she mourns the
loss of her son, denied first-rate hospital treatment after a sawmill
accident three years before. Aibileen's maternal casting amounts to
a southern version of the busty fertility figures that were humanity's
first figurative art, carved from mammoth teeth thirty-five thousand
years ago.

In *The Second Sex*, published in 1949, Simone de Beauvoir writes
of how women are a blank canvas for the imagination: "Nurse, guide,
judge, mediatrix, mirror, woman is the Other in whom the subject
transcends himself." The southern Black maid is a related arche-
type in history's long list of feminine projections, a specific subset
of the Other. De Beauvoir maintained that the maternal figure—a
woman like Aibileen and her literary clones—"is so necessary to
man's happiness and to his triumph that it can be said that if she did
not exist, men would have invented her." In *The Second Sex*—which
eventually landed on the Catholic Church's list of banned books—de
Beauvoir draws parallels between the limits and projections placed
on women and on the Jim Crow experiences of expatriate writer
Richard Wright, her Jackson-reared friend.

Stockett's novel may be the most popular entry in the genre of
fiction that explores the tension between midcentury Black maids
and their white employers, but it's not the only take on the topic.
The dynamic is examined in two other Mississippi works, the late
Ellen Douglas's *Can't Quit You, Baby* (1988) and Minrose Gwin's
The Queen of Palmyra (2010). Each narrative proffers a sharper-
eyed, unsentimental examination of the lopsided maid-employer tie.
Like *The Help*, these novels also feature southern kitchens in brisk
use: tomato aspic, exemplary roasts, and six kinds of cakes (from
thin-layered lemon to dense devil's food) come with the literary
territory. *Can't Quit You, Baby* demonstrates how decades' worth
of suppressed anger can underlie an outwardly smooth relationship. In *The Queen of Palmyra*, the maid's connection to her white
employers unwittingly facilitates a Black death. In both novels, the

antagonists come with painful histories that somewhat explain their flawed actions and draw reader empathy.

The Queen of Palmyra is set near Jackson, and the clearest gaze in the story belongs to Zenie Johnson, a housemaid whose work makes her a bridge between the white and Black communities of the fictional town of Millwood in the pivotal summer of 1963 (the same setting as *The Help*). Zenie Johnson has a survivor's intuition; her insights confirm standpoint theory, which holds that less powerful people in a group inevitably have a clearer and more objective read of a situation than the powerful at the center because the marginalized can't afford not to see reality. Zenie reluctantly agrees to lodge her outspoken college niece for the summer. Just as unenthusiastically, she consents to having her employer's granddaughter Florence come to her home in the afternoons until the child's father, Win, can pick her up. Win is a third-generation Klansman who, in terms of his horrible family tradition, initially seems more sentimental than threatening. He stores his robe in a treasured-heirloom wooden box and for a while manages to retain a measure of good will with readers. Meanwhile, Win's wife, Martha, unravels over her husband's Klan affiliation. She eventually runs away in the family's dented red Chevy. At that point, Zenie is who sees how dire life is for the terrified, silent Florence. In a Dostoevskian way, the novel tracks how disassociation grows in Florence's traumatized mind; the more horrific Win becomes, the less his once canny, now neglected and abused daughter absorbs what is going on around her. Win's demons psychologically sicken his bystanding family.

In *Can't Quit You, Baby*, the villain turns out to be the book's satisfied and serene protagonist: forty-four-year-old Cornelia O'Kelly. She manages nicely with her growing deafness, often preferring to turn off her hearing aid to enjoy the silence. Her 1969 household is a display of genteel eye candy; her suitably shining walnut dining table is spread nightly with equally suitable from-scratch dinners. Around the living room, carefully cropped family photos are on silver-framed display. Cooking alongside her housekeeper, Tweet

Carrier, Cornelia prides herself on being sensitive and conscientious enough to feign interest in Tweet's affable, long-winded accounts of past family failures. Yet Cornelia only pretends to listen. She doesn't care about Tweet's pain, nor does she dwell on her own wounded-ness. The steely Cornelia has neither the emotional bravery nor the generosity to listen. As the novel progresses, Cornelia comes to realize that all her intimates resent her rigid curation of reality. As the chief relationships of her life come into question, she faces how flawed human ties inevitably are—and how recalibration is often possible instead of rupture, a truth Tweet has always known. After Tweet's husband betrayed her, Tweet shot him. Two wrongs may not make a right, but the literal bloodshed rearranged the dynamics between her husband and herself, Tweet notes. Adopting Tweet's approach, Cornelia seeks to reset her connection to Tweet, which is as metaphorically bleeding as Tweet's unfaithful husband once was at Tweet's hands. "What can we do . . . when we've shot somebody?" Cornelia comes to ask Tweet in hopes of reconciliation. "Look around? See where we're headed? That's all I can see to do after you shoot somebody." The approach presumes there's no escaping some kind of connection as long as both are breathing.

The maid characters created by Douglas and Gwin are both child-less, strategically defying the nurturing maternal Black stereotype; neither Zenie Johnson in *The Queen of Palmyra* nor Tweet Carrier in *Can't Quit You, Baby* ooze much warmth. Far from being a country-rooted earth mother, Tweet is repelled by newly hatched chicks. They seem more sinister than endearing to her; she is unnerved by the soft, almost absent quality of their bones.

Devoid of the Madonna mantle, the characters bristle with what Margaret Mead identified as "post-menopausal zest." The wise woman, crone, or hag—all recognizable identities across cultures—is a persona who rises up as a figure of authority at the close of a woman's fertile years. Tweet and Cornelia exude strength. (Zenie's full name is Zenobia, in tribute to the ancient queen of Palmyra who eventually ruled Egypt and successfully led an army against the Roman Empire.) In fact, they do not traffic in traditional feminine beauty. Each has a markedly marred appearance that has developed in middle age: Zenie has weeping leg sores underneath her thick work stockings, while Tweet's facial "risings" are suggested in a factor in her husband's infidelity.

There is a deeper underlying connection between the two books. Gwin has been a longtime teacher of southern literature at the University of North Carolina at Chapel Hill and is devoted to the works of Douglas as well as those of Mississippi-born novelist Elizabeth Spencer. She admires both for their groundbreaking examinations of racial injustice from the white perspective dating from the 1950s and early 1960s. When I asked her about these two influences in writing *The Queen of Palmyra*, Gwin told me, "I was always trying to live up to their subtlety and their piercing moments of insight."

In Jackson, now with an 82.8 percent Black population, I've noticed that when anyone I know hires a house cleaner these days, the worker is either white or Hispanic (groups that account for 14.5 and 1.5 percent of the population, respectively). A friend of mine counsels adolescents, and she occasionally hears a Black teenager say their grandmother worked as a maid and forbids her grandchildren from ever considering doing so, the job that the US Department of Labor classifies as "Private Household Occupations." History makes the prospect a nonstarter.

As for me, I occasionally employ Judy Anderson, who is forty-four, white, and in a college accounting class with someone I know. She comes to work in Bermuda shorts, with earbuds peeping through her long blonde hair; as she reorganizes my hall closet and garage, she listens to motivational podcasts on her phone. She always departs in time for her evening gig as a Fitness Lady cardio instructor. She charges twenty-five an hour. I've never worried about the subtext of our relationship.

On one of my recent insulin runs, I asked Mrs. Sanders if she would give me her honest thoughts on working for me, however unflattering. Given the longtime limits on our candor with each other, this was a fairly stilted attempt at getting at the truth. Still, maybe she had less to lose at that point.

Leaning on her walker, Mrs. Sanders opened the front door of her mauve brick ranch house. She had started construction on her house before her late husband received his cancer diagnosis. After his death in 1984, she pressed ahead with the house—on a cash basis over the span of a few years—until she eventually moved into her new four-bedroom home mortgage-free.

Inside, she led me through the foyer, past the living room, and into the open kitchen-den area. I've always noticed that every table surface in the household has a spotless luster, as do her oak floors. My house never gleamed like that, not when Mrs. Sanders was clean-ing it, and certainly not now that I do the cleaning myself. That fact never ceased to miff me. How it bothered me is evidence that my skull housed an entitled hotspot.

Mrs. Sanders slid the sack of six boxed insulin bottles into her refrigerator, then we settled on the nearby sofa. She had on black pants and a jade paisley tunic with an *S* monogrammed over her heart.

"You know, I always paid you forty dollars," I began. "That was a long time for you to go without a raise. But I paid you when I was out of town, and I'd add twenty some weeks. I told myself it evened out." I was begging a little.

Mrs. Sanders nodded. "You did." Her encouraging smile was as congenial as always.

"Still, I let myself off the hook on giving you a real raise." There was a tiny hitch in my voice.

Maybe my intrusion and belated frankness made Mrs. Sanders feel uncomfortable, too. Maybe she felt sorry for me and wanted to make me feel better. Whatever the reason, at that point Mrs. Sanders shifted back to our old conversational comfort zone: the failures of Barbara.

"That was the worst family I ever worked for," she said. Mrs. Sand-ers never pressed me for a raise, but she did at Barbara's, she said; Mrs. Sanders had insisted on ten dollars an hour. "I had to tell her the facts." She also noted that since she stopped working for Barbara, the woman had visited her house only twice, once bringing a silk flower in a thumb-sized metal bud vase. She never brought a gift of extra cash. "I meant nothing to her," Mrs. Sanders said. The bridge of her nose folded into slashes of disdain.

"I never knew what other people paid," I continued. "You didn't say, and I didn't ask."

"I knew you were a single person," said Mrs. Sanders.

"How did what I paid compare to what other people paid?"

Mrs. Sanders paused. Then she went ahead with it. "It was on the low side."

I guess I always knew that.

"I thought about a raise, but you were a nice lady. You might have been pressed." She looked me in the eye. She didn't wear the pink opaline-rimmed glasses anymore. Her new frames were silver metal. "I knew you were a single parent. That means you have to see about everything. Good, kind treatment is better than money."

If that's true, my urge to examine my long relationship to Mrs. Sanders might reveal another possibility. Am I flattering myself by digging into the Old South myth, however bad it makes me look? Maybe I am socioeconomically overrating myself. Am I exaggerating the importance of my subpar pay on Tuesdays? Did it matter so much one way or the other? The reality is that Mrs. Sanders and I have plenty in common: we are both single women who own ranch houses in Jackson, each of us mother to a pair of college-graduate offspring. Maybe my guilt is a backdoor means of self-aggrandizement.

In my exploration of the employer-housemaid nexus, I've discovered a fact that shouldn't have surprised me but did: it is white women who write most specifically about the relationship. When Black women write about characters who are housemaids, they treat the job as one component of a larger story, not the sun around which the pages spin (Sofia in *The Color Purple* hates her job, for example, and Mississippi-born poet Natasha Trethewey writes about her grandmother's Sunday-morning off-hour in "Domestic Work, 1937"). Barbara Neely's Blanche White detective series centers on the sleuthing exploits of a tart middle-aged woman who works as a domestic. Playwright Alice Childress's 1956 collection *Like One of the*

Family features the maid Mildred Johnson in her off-hours, archly telling her Harlem neighbor Marge, also a maid, about her day job's indignities. Of course, white writers hone in on the work hours of maids because that time is the intersection that exists between the white and Black characters. The unnamed narrator of Ellen Douglas's *Can't Quit You, Baby* says so. "I thought I was at home in Tweet's life, that when she spoke, I heard her speak with her own authentic voice," she observes. "But of course I never heard her speak, except to Cornelia. Does that trouble you as it does me?" And there are other reasons why the employer-employee relationship might matter more from the white woman's point of view. Hiring a maid represented a rare act of economic agency for white women up until the last few decades. For generations, what happened inside a white woman's house was, for the most part, nearly her whole story.

The early psychoanalyst Karen Horney challenged her mentor Sigmund Freud in the 1920s over his male-centric theories as applied to the lives of women. Women's behavior, development, and longings were richer and broader than simply a response to a male world, she reported in lectures and papers from 1922 until 1936. Yet she shifted her efforts by the late 1930s. The realities and habits of the wider culture were so knotted into the choices and behavior of women—and men—that it was impossible to separate a culture's stamp from what was innate and true inside any one person's head. Humans move in a unified field fused with the place and time where they are.

I think about Mrs. Sanders between my visits to her house, but it's a relief that she no longer comes to mine. I'd rather economize, and I don't just mean in terms of keeping my forty dollars and plowing the Swiffer down my own hall. It's an economical choice in terms of mental payload. Maybe an analysis of race doesn't have to hijack a simple decision to pay someone to sweep the floor. But inside my fifty-seven-year-old head in Jackson, it still does.

Chapter 11

Are You a Seg Academy Alum, Too? Let's Talk

THE STAKES WERE HIGH IN 1970 WHEN DEEP SOUTH SCHOOL desegregation transformed the region's classrooms, stadiums, and teacher lounges into America's most integrated, at least for a while. A few months before, the Supreme Court had called a halt to nearly two decades of post-1954 *Brown* stonewalling. Racial history shifted in one sweep: Black and white, children and educators. Lives changed. Old patterns shattered. The transformation, wrapped in clear historic moral purpose, affected over 11 million children.

And then there were us. I'm one of the estimated 750,000 Deep South white alumni of the segregation academies that sprouted up in eleven states to defy the ideal of racial equality.

Films like the Virginia-set *Remember the Titans* and *The Best of Enemies*, based on Durham, North Carolina, events, center on that hard-won moment of public school transformation in the seventies. The academies' parallel stories? We don't talk about it much. In fact, we alums prefer skipping over our high school histories due to the potential for blowback that the truth of our all-white alma maters provokes now. In Mississippi, US Senator Cindy Hyde-Smith's 1977 graduation from Lawrence County Academy ballooned into a campaign issue in the 2018 Senate race after a *Jackson Free Press* report brought on national attention. Former governor Phil Bryant has stated that he attended Jackson Public Schools, yet he spent his final years at McCluer Academy, graduating in 1973.

The fact is, however, that our academy bona fides matter in far more scenarios than the unlikely one of a run for office. Our academy educations matter all the time. They matter not just in terms of what people ought to know about us, but, just as importantly, in what we know—or dare to confront—about ourselves. Outwardly, we look okay, right? Right?

It's over-Faulknerfied to say so, but the past's not past, certainly not for white academy alums living and engaging in the twenty-first century. Our story is not just history but an unfolding question: how does our defiant schooling inadvertently still shape us and our heads by default? It does, of course, in unconscious and conscious ways.

Among Mississippi academy alums aren't just ruby-red officeholders like Hyde-Smith in Washington and Bryant, who spent eight years in the governor's mansion. Other Mississippians who've made a national mark in the culture came out of white academies too. These include actor Sela Ward (Lamar School, 1973) and blockbuster novelists Donna Tartt (Kirk Academy, 1981) and Kathryn Stockett (Jackson Preparatory School, 1987). Author Steve Yarbrough graduated from Indianola Academy in 1975, CNN anchor Shepard Smith from Marshall Academy, while writer-journalist Neely Tucker ruled as Mr. Starkville Academy (1982). Britney Spears and Jamie Lynn Spears attended Parklane Academy in McComb. Let the record reflect that I was in the Pillow Academy Class of 1974 Hall of Fame. Hyde-Smith's segregation academy was about 150 miles south of mine. Bryant's academy in Jackson used to play mine in football. (In my memory, McCluer parents were famous for spoiling for a postgame fight with our parents.)

In Mississippi, our cohort represented an estimated 43,278 white children who disappeared from the state's public schools to enter private ones as integration took hold in earnest. In 1964, the state had less than twenty private schools. The number ballooned to 236 by 1971.

I enrolled at Pillow Academy in January 1970, the moment when, due to the ruling in *Alexander v. Holmes County Board of Education*, thirty-three Mississippi school districts, including our Delta town's, were directed by the US Supreme Court to cease fifteen years of post-*Brown* delay. Schools were to reopen after winter break fully integrated. In some districts, white students were told to take their public school textbooks home at Christmas to use at their new academy in January.

I'm certain the all-white academy experience left its mark on me. It did on the others, too. If Hyde-Smith's and Bryant's records show racist antagonism—and they do—they came out of high schools founded on exactly that. Race plays into the works of Mississippi novelists who come out of the academies as well, either by confronting white supremacy or sometimes by simply producing work in which whiteness can't help but come through. Sometimes both.

My academy was a cream-yellow prefabricated steel building in a cotton field near the Mississippi town of Greenwood. My parents and parents of my eighth-grade friends plucked us from our public school ahead of the approaching Black-enrollment increase. My friends and I hated Pillow Academy at first. Not because we were racially enlightened—I won't insult you with a cover-up story—but because the school was surprisingly big and chaotic. We were simply unhappy at being deposited into the raw new building outside the city limits with white strangers from five-or-so counties. Our former oak-shaded blond-brick Greenwood public school had been familiar and better equipped with features like a cafeteria and a feeling of belonging. Everyone in that era in the South, Black and white, all 11 million of us who were school age, has a story on how our path shifted. In that way, we did have a shared experience—the only common interracial one for those of us in the academies.

Back then, I felt bad about my new school's obvious purpose. I silently fretted that I'd be asked point-blank what school I attended by someone who was Black. I cringed at the insult my answer represented. I needn't have worried over a conversation so unlikely; despite living in the Mississippi Delta—an area with the highest proportion of Black residents of any region of the country—I never actually knew one Black teen in my town of twenty-three thousand, surreal as that sounds. That was an immediate byproduct of academy schooling, one that, of course, limits the stock of life experiences I had available to draw from as an adult.

At the outpost in the Delta field, my seventies high school years were average in some ways: the Jackson Five and Gladys Knight as a soundtrack (interestingly, Motown was the top choice, white rockers second tier), shag haircuts, and repeated reads of the Sonny Corleone sex scene in *The Godfather* paperback. Before long, the new academy developed school trappings like a photography club and valentine dance as niceties beyond the school's bedrock racist mission. If my friends and I hated moving to the academy initially, we eventually settled in. It was our one and only version of the high school experience. The teachers were as well intentioned in the classroom as most. No one teaches to get rich, academy faculty included. While some teachers had fled to the academy to sidestep integration, other teachers landed there simply because they needed a job, and the academy was hiring.

Inside, I can't say there were even any overt conversations about the school's white supremacist purpose. It hardly needed to be articulated, though; it was handled by the euphemistic, loaded explanation that Pillow had been established for "a quality education." So did so many other schools. Even now on checking academies' websites, there's the usual explanation that their town came to feel a need for a "quality" private school in the year—surprise—1970.

Outside the official messaging, weekend vandalism in town shouted in loud paint. In a history of Mississippi school desegregation titled *Just Trying to Have School*, Mary Carol Miller remembered Pillow Academy boys coming to integrated Greenwood High on weekends, painting N—TECH on the parking-lot pavement. In turn, Greenwood High students sneaked on to the Pillow grounds to scrawl REDNECK TECH, she said.

To be fair, what we learned in Pillow history class was distorted, true, but so was public school curriculum then as well: enslaved people had enjoyed good treatment, and Reconstruction—the brief years when Black Mississippians held office and voted in substantial numbers—was an era of white suffering like the Civil War itself. None of us heard a word about the lynching of Emmett Till in our hometown's backyard, although the visiting Chicago teen's murder had drawn international coverage in 1955 and launched the civil rights movement. When I finally heard about the Till case—I was twenty-five, living 260 miles away, and it was the eighties—I recognized the last names of classmates I'd known whose elders had been in law enforcement or led the winning defense of Till's murderers. After their acquittal, the murderers confessed for *Look* magazine. Bryant's Grocery, the site where Till allegedly flirted with the owner, was nine miles straight up County Road 518 from my former public school.

Here's the aftermath of academy bona fides, I think: the imperative to gauge how the thinking bred in such a school—along with growing up inside a white society that invested huge energy into the segregation academy's creation—lingers inside the head still, even if switched on silent. We were conscientiously and misguidedly furnished an unbending white universe. I wonder how the region and all of us academy stamped would have been different if an alternative had happened, and locals had worked to invest fully in the public schools and making them work. Instead, I'm uncertain I can ever completely disconnect the old white-centered framework inside deep places in my head. The point of our rigid academy schooling and parallel existence was to keep us blind to all beyond it. This blocks you from knowing what you don't know. Minds that result from an immersion like that are like the baffled fish in the parable: when asked how's the water, the fish asks, "What's water?" The fish can't grasp what's distinctive about its surroundings—comprehensively white, in my case.

A 1971 research paper released by the Southern Regional Council on segregation academies said as much: "Many of these new schools, with their underlying philosophy of 'Never!' are a warping influence on the children who attend. Even aside from the implications of removing children to a segregated situation in a democratic country, it is important to note that many of these schools are motivated by an extremely right-wing philosophy which in the name of 'patriotism' and 'quality education' is a perversion of the nation's ideals."

When it comes to turning up photographs of blackface dress-up in the past of current white politicians, I get their capacity for tone-deaf oblivion. It was a byproduct of our school years, a time when the laws had changed but many white heads didn't intend to. Rather than receiving a "quality education," the truth was that our shut-away school ensured our ignorance to all beyond our white lock-in in the middle of a field.

During that 2018 Senate campaign, Hyde-Smith also made head-lines for joking about a public hanging as she ran to represent the state with the highest number of documented lynchings in US history. As for Bryant, he invited the polarizing President Trump to the Mississippi Civil Rights Museum's 2017 opening, setting off a first-day boycott by Black supporters, including the late civil rights icon US Rep. John Lewis of Georgia. While Bryant's stunt came across as openly hostile, sometimes our peer group's skulls simply hold store loads of free-floating white blindness and associated contortions that need unpacking.

Here's an episode to share in the case of my claimed silent disapproval over my school's racist rationale. It turned out that it didn't count for much for me on ninth-grade Mississippi History Day. When we were assigned to dress up to salute the state's past, I had what I thought a funny idea. I dug in the hall closet at home for a double bedsheet to go as a Ku Klux Klansman. I lacked both the moral empathy and even the acquaintance with a Black person to fathom that the costume choice was not fun but appalling. Then again, my wardrobe selection was a crystal-pure reflection of my education. It said more than my ninth-grade academy report card ever could. I failed to think about how, six years before, three young civil rights volunteers had been captured and murdered by Klansmen ninety-odd miles away in Neshoba County. I paraded down the concrete school hall with classmates in blander gingham settler costumes. No one called me on the outfit—not my parents nor any teacher or classmate. They were as heedless—and white—as me. I think I remember the school custodian, African American, silently looking at my flowing getup in the hall. Or do I? Was his gaze an imagined guilty memory, the human rendering of a faint tremor in my conscience?

Recently I pulled my yearbooks off the high top shelf. Inevitably it was there when I looked: a blackface photo. Page 150 of the 1972 volume. It featured a trio of boys in gooey face paint, wigs, and cheerleader dresses. Maybe from a pep rally skit when we all hooted and clapped.

Like Confederate memorials or a still-standing plantation home on tour, legacy segregation academies remain part of the southern landscape. My alma mater, like most others, now has a small Black enrollment and official nondiscrimination policies. On National Signing Day in February 2019, one of the nation's top high school prospects was Jerrion Ealy, now of the Kansas City Chiefs, then a Black senior at Jackson Preparatory School, the Mississippi capital city's most prestigious segregated private school at its 1970 founding. Greenville Christian School, founded in 1969, has morphed into having a 75 percent Black enrollment and the leading football team, all Black, in academy play.

Reading Jackson native Angie Thomas's blockbuster book *The Hate U Give*, I wondered if Williamson Prep was a disguised Jackson Prep as the book's protagonist Starr Carter spends her time code-switching between her Black neighborhood Garden Heights and her nearly all-white private school. Thomas told me Williamson isn't modeled on any particular school, but *The Hate U Give* "can provide a glimpse into the way those schools operate and the environment they provide for Black students."

When Pillow Academy commemorated the fiftieth anniversary of its opening a few years ago, there was only a single mention in the thirty-six-page commemorative section in the *Greenwood Commonwealth* that inched near the white supremacist reality of Pillow's start. The line noted vaguely and absurdly that the all-white school opened when "throughout the South, citizens of both races were concerned about the volatility of forced desegregation." In truth, one of the founders of the academy was also the founder of the Citizens' Council, the national white supremacy organization that Pulitzer-winning journalist Hodding Carter declared the "uptown Klan" operating in hundreds of southern towns. His role as founder of both is included in Robert "Tut" Patterson's 2017 obituary.

The hometown conversation that I'd feared as a fifteen-year-old finally took place this year, but instead of dodging it, I initiated it. I asked a Black Greenwood contemporary what he had thought of the academy back in our parallel high school days. Sylvester Hoover said Pillow Academy had been in operation for a few years before he even knew it existed. He was as unaware of the academy just outside the city limits as I was of him; back then, I'm ashamed to say, Sylvester Hoover would have been only a vaguely personified idea to me, one which my white culture told me represented a threat to my education and even my safety.

I left Greenwood at age eighteen. Hoover didn't. He runs Delta Blues Legends Tours there, sharing local history with visitors. One of the main stops on his tour is the beautiful country church Little Zion Missionary Baptist, built by its members in 1871. It's Hoover's lifelong congregation and the site of the church-sanctuary scene in *The Help*. Bluesman Robert Johnson is buried in the cemetery on the grounds. Hoover's tour continues to Bryant's Grocery in Money where Emmett Till's candy purchase led to his murder.

Hoover has a nephew who recently graduated from Pillow Academy. Hoover himself would have no problem sending a child there, he said. He's mulled touching base with the academy to offer to present his local history talk. "I bet they'd say yes," he said. Mississippi and those of us here continue to surprise each other.

Token integration at the still-surviving academies isn't a shocker. Lip service to racial equality is as much a part of the current South as Whole Foods, Apple, and H&M locations, of course. Yet racism obscured can't be confronted. That's the problem in leaving my high school alma mater blank on my resume, as lots of academy alums do, aware of the stakes of its messaging in the wider world.

I don't list my high school on my Facebook profile. I want to dodge Black acquaintances finding out that chunk of my past. Yet in truth, my academy story must be part of any honest account of my whole story. For me to shove aside those academy years is indulging in a timeline hideout, a personal-history version of tucking myself behind the entrance of a gated community when it comes to reckoning with race.

Privilege permits dodges like that, insulation from the discomfort of reckoning with the racist components in my life and thinking, conscious and unconscious. Yet that protection from being forced to expose yourself also means a lost opportunity potentially to learn to do and think better. That's the assertion of the book *White Fragility: Why It's So Hard for White People to Talk About Racism* by Robin DiAngelo.

My high school experience clings to my present like so much gooey pep rally face paint. The upside is that an easy-read past like mine clearly means its stamp is there if I'm willing to breathe and take a look. Claiming you've never been less than fair minded and egalitarian is for people with less extreme histories than mine—or my cohort's. Hard questions ought to be the obligatory surcharge to our alumni dues.

My Pillow Academy Class of 1974 motto actually zeroed in on the kind of self-scrutiny academy alums are compelled to consider. In lofty typeface, jumping up off the gloss of the page of our senior yearbook, I see our class motto: "God asks no man whether he will accept life. . . . The only choice is how."

That isn't so far from the truth.

Part 3

A Steps Miscellany

Chapter 12

Volunteering (3)

TO TELL THE TRUTH, I WOULD HAVE ASKED ME, TOO. THE CHURCH needed a volunteer to head Meals on Wheels on the second Thursday of the month. I had a responsible-enough past record: I'd taught Sunday school and Bible school, ladled lunch in the soup kitchen serving line, and arrived on the right day every year with the right pink bike for the church Christmas toy drive. Combine that with the deal-closing fact that Gus and I had just renovated a circa 1940 two-story lager-yellow clapboard house with a big-ass kitchen island. Not long after the move, our St. Andrew's priest Molly MacWade came by. She shot more than an idle eye around the bright yellow kitchen with shiny black granite countertops. In her warm honey voice, she asked if I'd start handling community Meals on Wheels on the second Thursday monthly. I felt my mouth say yes.

So at age forty-one, Meals on Wheels rolled into my life as involuntarily as the fresh loose skin folds started to bunch under my eyes. Neither were welcome. MOW felt like one more signal of my arrival at a new life phase. If I didn't know I was becoming a middle-aged woman, Meals on Wheels was there to tell me. In the church-job timeline for women, first comes the young mom pitching in for 11 a.m. children's church in a cute floaty Sunday dress and, for one week in the summer, rocking a sheet, sandals, and arm bracelet as an Egyptian group leader for Bible school. But the subsequent meat loaf makers and milk buyers of Meals on Wheels? The menopause adjacent, assigned to their kitchens.

The only life stage remaining after a Meals on Wheels job is receiving Meals on Wheels yourself. Several hardworking, longtime former MOW cake bakers and coleslaw providers were now on the delivery list. In fact, I was replacing a stalwart who had become disabled and was scooting directly behind the MOW velvet rope, avoiding the recipient waiting list. Behold the flow of your years, my new volunteer duty said to me. The dough in my abdomen where muscle used to be wiggled a nod of agreement.

Besides being an indicator of aging, the project struck me as just as sexist as the altar guild. How many men does the church ask to cook on a weekday or, on the altar guild, polish chalices and launder Communion linens as God's housewife? Midlife women are buttonholed as MOW meal jockeys, the natural go-tos to feed not only family members but two routes of other people as well. It's only eighteen more mouths, the assumption seemed to be. Of course MOW was meaningful work, but it would be even more meaningful by packing the message that the support of the old and ill was everyone's job, not solely of over-forty women.

I got to work begrudgingly. One night after supper, Gus listened in the kitchen while I moved down the call list of the ten volunteer cooks, confirming they remembered to bring their meat, vegetable, bread, dessert, and milk by 10 a.m. the upcoming Thursday.

Hanging near the kitchen island, which still gave off our house's new paint smell, Gus said, "Of all the work you do, this makes me proudest."

What an odd, irritating read, I thought, loading supper plates into the dishwasher between cook calls. What was his comment really about?

"You think so?" I said out loud, wiggling the next greasy plate into the bottom dishwasher rack, the aftermath of the night's baked chicken breasts, green salad, and broccoli. Postsupper, Molly and Kate headed upstairs, shutting their doors.

"It's great that you're doing this," he said. Still in his work clothes, Gus poured another glass of sauvignon blanc. I tensed, my cortisol edging up. He moved toward his green chair by the TV. The kitchen and den were one big bright yellow room due to knocking out walls in the remodel. He clicked the remote for ESPN and cranked up the recliner footrest.

Why did Gus approve of the Meals on Wheels gig for me so much? I suspected he liked the nurture-packed messaging: me as a bloodless, need-free Angel in the House, the modern version of that Victorian projection. But I didn't ask.

That lack of follow-up showcased the store load of resignation in the back of my skull back then. I sprinted past any issue when I thought the odds of change were low. Instead of calling out either MOW, or, more personally, how Gus now emptied a bottle of Mondavi nightly and vanished inside a thin-skinned fog I hated, I said zilch about either. I'd confront him over mean-drunk episodes—he had a few a year—challenging him to reconsider being a drinker at all. He'd apologize for the word spews of the night before but drew the line in the marital sand over quitting.

I never turned his drinking into a deal breaker, because I knew it would be. I was certain. We'd been together two decades. I loved him long and hard, along with the life that had shaped around that fact of us. Did I really want to decide that the original Gus was missing now, never to return? If so, I'd be choosing to become an exhausted single working mother with a home front double shift. Millions of women did so, having no choice. I did—if I kept my mind's alignment just right. There's that Robert Frost line about freedom as "being easy in your harness." I floated past what I didn't like, including dwelling too long on my marital uneasiness. Gus and I still had more fun in our genuine good times than lots of couples in lower-friction unions.

So that night, Meals on Wheels–wise, I logically chalked up Gus as simply one more human who found it handy to shunt me into the world of giving women who are Meals on Wheels years old. The world always has relied on unobtrusive women in the kitchen for the rest of the population to function. Just because I was an at-home mother and spouse, admittedly a sweet gig most of the time, I didn't consider myself a task dumpster for the population at large. I kept Gus's books, fed and ferried family, and showed up prn for them. I was part of a Tuesday-morning girls' club at Hardy Middle School, a volunteer gig I sought out for my Junior League job for the year. I generally thought my time had value. It was my call on how to divvy it up, however, not others' with their whims and suspect projections.

Once the dishwasher was rumbling, I filled supper bowls—naturally I was the one who did—for our retrievers Sonny and Molasses. The roar of the ESPN basketball game looped the yellow room. Gus nodded off in the recliner. Minutes later, Gus's snore joined the blare of ESPN basketball on the TV.

Calls done, dogs fed, I went upstairs. I passed the girls' bedroom doors. I could hear Kate talking on her phone. Voices from a Disney show came out of Molly's room. Once settled alone in bed, I sipped a nightcap glass of sauvignon blanc myself and read my night's page count of fiction. Then I turned out the light.

MOW Menu: Ham with Jezebel Sauce, Turnip Greens, Broccoli, Beaten Biscuits

Working with other humans is a revelation into who they are, of course. But seeing what they choose to cook and how they pull it off? The equivalent of a vivisection. It turned out that two Meals on Wheels cogs were kicks: Eleanor Fontaine and Tay Wise, pillar St. Andrew's parishioners and MOW cooks. Before there were Brangelina and Javanka, there was Tayleanor, at least for me.

No-nonsense Eleanor Fontaine had short gray hair, front-buttoning, collared white cotton blouses, and Wellesley credentials. Tall and unflappable, she folded a big sense of duty into her MOW bread batter. If you looked into her calm face for more than a moment, you saw the live wattage shooting out from underneath those octogenarian eyelids. She took in the world and then responded in loaded and surprisingly limited words.

Meals on Wheels was a priority for her. She'd turned out sticker-decorated Ziplocs of home baking on second Thursdays for years. She'd telephone. "Ellen Ann? Are you home? John could bring the

bread to you." She still had her hybrid Missouri-Wellesley pronunciation along with an old tan Buick station wagon and fifties ranch
built by her husband, John, a Harvard design alum. Architects in
town salivated over their low-slung mod house, a few blocks from
mine. Inside twenty-five-hundred-odd square feet were four bed-
rooms, three children, sheet glass, brick walls, and an interior Bud-
dhist garden east of the dining room. For sixty years, the Fontaines
lived there at the end of a cul-de-sac. The house's traits described
Eleanor herself: unshowy yet extraordinary once you thought about
it. She'd been part of Wednesdays in Mississippi, a 1960s under-
ground biracial exchange between hats-and-gloves northern women
and their Mississippi counterparts to advance civil rights. Only a
scant handful of Jackson white women took the economic and
social-ostracism risk of taking part. Eleanor was one who did. To
be clear, for most Jackson white women, it wasn't a fraught, regretful
weighing of risk; they were simply as big of white supremacists as
the men and rejected any part of it.

Most months, Eleanor made beaten biscuits for Meals on Wheels.
She switched to cranberry scones at Christmas and hot cross buns
at Easter. Her Ziploc stickers were month appropriate: shamrocks
in March, the American flag in July. Every month, John brought the
Ziplocs in a plastic grocery sack to my porch. One of the reasons
for Eleanor's circumspection was John's counterbalancing role as
their front-of-the-house person. Lots of his airtime, though, went
to lauding how Eleanor rolled. He once published a weekly column
in the local *Northside Sun* going over Eleanor's weekly household
management. She believed in old-school laundry on Monday and a
weekly lamb-chop night. If only every home had Eleanor in charge,
John reflected. Hard to argue, I thought.

Tay Wise was Eleanor's match and, unsurprisingly, her good
friend. Tay was gray-haired, short, and round. I don't mean fat. I
mean her face was circular, and within it, along with her pleasant small smile, her round eyes were the same kind of observa-
tion lagoons as Eleanor's. Her oversized rimless glasses, also round,
were the final concentric note. Tay grew up in Canton, twenty miles

outside of Jackson. She'd graduated from then all-girls' Belhaven College in Jackson as a music major and the May Queen. On graduation she married Sherwood Wise, a bachelor lawyer who took civic life as seriously as she did.

Tay was a MOW meat cook. When I made the monthly heads-up call to Tay, she didn't pause for niceties. "Meat or chicken?" she asked with urgency. When she picked a cause, it orbited her mind. Circles penetrated down to an inner mindset theme of Tay's as well.

In violation of my initial MOW St. Andrew's management instructions, I dispensed with keeping up with when we served what. Month-to-month meat monitoring struck me as undue mental load begging to be chucked as part of the job. I hesitated.

"It's meat this month, isn't it?" Tay said.

"It sure is," I confirmed. It was if Tay said so.

Tay had more than a half century as a volunteer under her belt, from every St. Andrew's church role possible, to 1952 Junior League president, to 1960 Jackson Symphony League president. Her do-good dedication provoked mean-woman gossip. It goaded frenemies years later that Tay simply didn't care that she still had seventies-issue pink shag carpet in her Eastover living room matting over time. What she cared about was her volunteer work, down to the monthly meat-or-chicken conundrum.

Since John was delivering her friend Eleanor's bread anyway, Tay buttonholed him to carpool her foil-wrapped trays of meat loaf and barbecued chicken pieces to me as well. My favorite Tay standard was her frequent foil pan of ham slices with little individual lidded plastic to-go containers of homemade Jezebel sauce tucked alongside. She cooked for MOW recipients as meticulously as for a party at her house. Same for Eleanor.

Like Jezebel sauce, Tay and Eleanor were reminders of an earlier era when life for a middle-class woman—white ones, to be precise—didn't include a paying job. Neither woman had ever had one. The same history didn't go for Black women, of course. Jackson and the rest of the country would have fallen apart without the paid work of Black women.

Lois Anderson, longtime housekeeper at Tay's house, was part of MOW prep as well. If she picked up the phone before Tay when I called, she skipped to the point too: "You're Meals on Wheels? Meat or chicken?"

At my house, Mrs. Sanders's morning sometimes fell on Meals on Wheels Thursday. While the two route drivers and I spooned food in foam trays, Mrs. Sanders looked on as she crossed back and forth through the kitchen with sheets from the dryer or with the dozenth dustpan of Sonny's and Molasses's fur tufts from the wood floors.

"You're doing a good thing," she said on a circuit through the kitchen. I took her approval to heart, in contrast to my suspicion over Gus's nod. Her validation rated as an exhale for me. This was Jackson, Mississippi, after all, site of the 1963-set novel *The Help*. It was two generations later, and I still squirmed at the white woman-Black woman housekeeping trope—but I didn't squirm enough to quit paying Mrs. Sanders and clean up myself.

Mrs. Sanders side-eyed the emptied jumbo cans of Glory-brand turnip greens on the countertop. "You can buy greens in cans?"

"They're seasoned right," I said defensively. "Come taste." One of the vegetable volunteers swore by them. I thought they were good.

"That's okay." Her diplomatic smile made her real opinion clear as she crossed the kitchen toward the stairs.

Despite my huff that Meals on Wheels inordinately dumped its work on age forty-plus women, I liked finding myself part of the legacy of women who have bonded via cooking's conversations and components—talking about food, shopping for food, cooking the food, gauging the food, serving up the food. Tayleanor, Lois Anderson, Mrs. Sanders, and I coalesced month by month in our own small repeat of the story.

When the day's lunch was ladled out and sacked, I headed out on the route B ride. Meals delivered, route B driver Berry and I pulled into Collins Dream Kitchen—more on Collins and the conversation there later. Mission accomplished for another month. Five minutes later, we were munching our Collins second-Thursday usuals. Mine was fried pork chops, black-eyed peas, and banana pudding. Back at my house, it was also the usual on second Thursdays: Mrs. Sanders was taking care of the mess I'd left behind. That was a repeat of the same old story too.

MOW Menu: Stewed Chicken, Potato Casserole, String Beans, Beaten Biscuits

The route A and B drivers, Frances Jean and Berry, and I filled the day's eighteen sacks on the counter. Each bag had one lidded Styrofoam tray of hot meat and vegetables, another tray of chilled salad and fruit, the Ziploc of Eleanor's bread, a smaller Styrofoam box of dessert, and a spare banana. Outside in my driveway, we split the bags between the two drivers' cars. The route list fluctuated due to moves, hospitalizations, and, sadly, deaths.

"Ready?" asked Berry. He was an upbeat, flush-faced architect turned real estate salesperson, new to St. Andrew's and Meals on Wheels. Men did occasionally volunteer for Meals on Wheels, overwhelmingly as drivers (which meant that when they handed the food to the waiting recipient, they were the ones thanked instead of the volunteer women who'd done the previous 95 percent of the work). Berry had a thatch of salt-and-pepper hair and little black nose glasses. There was a bouncy friendliness to him, and I liked riding along. The stewed chicken and string bean smell in the back of the SUV made my stomach rumble.

Turning left off my street, we passed a melon brick house with a pediment over the front door and a fringe of palmettos. There was a sign from Nix-Tann, Berry's agency, in the grass.

"Know anyone who wants to buy a house?" Berry asked. He looked at the road ahead as he steered. "You gotta keep asking. It's people, and it's contacts." He was self-coaching as much as telling me. It was true that the perpetual top agents in town were high visibility in open-air Jackson. They took pains to be at every museum and AIDS fundraiser and at church. The women agents filled day- and nighttime tennis teams. People selected an agent from their acquaintance network, not a stranger's name printed on a random free coozie. Done with what a drafting table did to his back in architectural jobs, Berry reincarnated himself in real estate. At its core, selling houses was an almost organic no-work way to make a living if you liked to talk to people, he explained. "You've got to talk about something, so why not talk about houses for sale?"

There's linguistic elegance in real estate people's talk loop. They need chitchat for the required social mingling, and houses for sale are newsworthy Jackson fishbowl stories: a divorce, a bankruptcy, a job move, a stranger come to town. Berry, father of a pair of young-adult sons, was coming off a divorce and in a new house himself. He'd also come out and found his way to St. Andrew's, which had a solid gay male membership. For generations, the music at Episcopal churches wouldn't have existed without gay men's contributions.

We came to our first house on the route, a white asbestos-shingle ranch in need of a power wash. A senior in a cotton housecoat poked her head out the kitchen door. "Good morning," she said.

Berry passed her the sack. I pulled a plastic bottle of milk out of my grocery bag of milk pints and handed it over. Making the delivery a one-two tag team gave me a job, but it also kept milk leaks off the meals. There'd been complaints.

"Thank you. See you next time," she said. We were one of eight different delivery teams she saw monthly. That made distinguishing any of us neither possible nor necessary. The sack handover served as a quick welfare check on the recipient as well, but no one invited us in to dally. They were ready to eat. Exception: route A driver Frances Jean had a recipient in Belhaven who regularly pressured Frances Jean to come in and listen to her sing and play the ukulele.

Berry stopped at the next residence on the list. Its dusty white siding, scant and forlorn shrubs, and front door burglar bars suggested the resident's income and energy were on the wane. A frail recipient in a navy sweatshirt and matching sweatpants took her bag and thanked us. At the next house, in similar condition, a nice man appeared at the crack in the door. On to a woman in a modest Belhaven Heights apartment complex, a faded mauve silk flower wreath on her door. The sound of a soap opera filtered out the threshold when she reached for her sack. Next we parked near the entry at St. Mark's Villa, a senior apartment complex attached to its namesake Episcopal church, founded in 1883, with a historically Black membership. Three recipients were residents here. One of the men was waiting for us in the lobby. The other two were on the second floor.

"It's open," called out one of the second-floor residents when Berry knocked. Inside his unit, a red-faced man with rivets of worry lines on his face rolled toward us. His legs amputated, his arms powered his wheelchair forward with big muscular shoves. "Thank you so much," he rasped in a smoker's voice, the sack on his lap. He backed up the wheels to make room to reshut the door.

We drove by the shadow of the state capitol. Next on the list was not only my favorite recipient but also the favorite of every other delivery team too. Mr. Hayes lived in a rooming house operating in a falling-down, converted, turn-of-the-century bungalow only a few blocks west of downtown. He was waiting outside on a vinyl-padded kitchen chair on the porch when we pulled up to the curb.

He stood at the sound of our SUV doors, his face and sightless eyes fixed forward, and said, "Well, good day, now."

"Hello Mr. Hayes! How are you today?" Berry pulled a sack out of the back of the SUV.

Mr. Hayes, in khaki work pants and a tucked plaid shirt, refrained from reaching his hands out right away as if he expected his meal. That was what our arrival meant, of course, but he was too polite to omit the niceties first.

"I have your lunch, Mr. Hayes. Do you want me to put it somewhere?" Berry said.

"Oh, I'll take it." Then his hand stretched in our direction, his fingers clasping around the folded top of the sack. "Thank you so much."

"And your milk, Mr. Hayes." I put the damp bottle in his other palm.

"Thank you, too, young lady." Young lady? More proof that Mr. Hayes was blind, I noted.

"You doing all right, Mr. Hayes?" Berry asked.

"Doing very well, very well indeed," he said with a pleasant nod.

Something was visibly wrong with Mr. Hayes's right thigh. It bulged under the khaki fabric of his work pants, triple the size of his other leg. Its worrisome looks weren't something to ask about in a perfunctory meal delivery, though.

"All right. See you next month, Mr. Hayes." Berry had the SUV keys in his palm as he headed down the concrete porch steps.

"Yes, indeed. Thank you folks so much." Mr. Hayes stayed on the porch, his glassy gaze angled toward our car until he heard the car doors slammed, and we drove away.

Our Supper Menu: Gourmet Pasta Casserole, Broccoli, Green Salad

Meals are usually more than meals. In the case of MOW deliveries, it was also that quick welfare check at the moment of the sack handover. For a family, a meal is a rite that binds one to another. Model families gather for dinner at night, so, by gum, that meant mine. I set my cooking bar sub–Ina Garten, but I did my part to keep Kroger in business. My supper standards were baked chicken breasts, sautéed crawfish over rice, and, at least once a week, Gourmet Pasta Casserole, a pretentiously named recipe from a CorningWare ad in *Redbook* magazine, which gave penne, meat sauce, rosemary, and sautéed mushrooms an elevated sound. It had almost become my signature weeknight dish.

A grocery stop and the prep took up most of the end of the afternoon. Lately I'd added one more to-do to my time frame, though: calling Gus's office to ease my mind that he was coming home sober. He no longer waited until returning home to start drinking. I'd call his office around 4 p.m. If his assistant Amy reported he'd already left, that was bad news. He wasn't due home until sixish, so that meant he'd headed to Hal and Mal's, where Jackson suits like him gathered for a cool postwork few.

Around six thirty, I heard his ink-blue Ford humming up the driveway to a stop. The screen door creaked, then the key clicked in the kitchen door lock.

"Anybody home?"

"Hey-ey." I was zapping Parmesan in the food processor. Hot vapor floated out of the sink as the waiting cooked broccoli dripped in the white colander.

Gus's light-brown hair and beard were starting to gray; his mustache remained light brown. He was Brooks Brothers enough to look serious, but he livened his suit up with a purple panda tie—something expensive and whimsical like Hermès, not a gag number from a mall kiosk.

There was droop in his lids behind the tortoise moons of his Polo glasses. Not good, I knew. He was smashed. Whenever his lids half-hid his eyes, it signaled he was wasted. It was as if he'd pulled down the garage door on the rest of the world to sequester inside a haze. When we hugged hello, the cigarette smell oozed out of the gray wool of his sports jacket. The instant-read whiff test confirmed the Hal and Mal's pit stop. My stomach tensed. I pretended all was as it should be, though. Making an issue would preemptively scuttle our night before it started. My goal was a nice night. Maybe I could keep the family-supper optics on track anyway.

"Where're the girls?" He looked around the yellow kitchen space, his question rhetorical, since if they weren't in the kitchen, they were upstairs. He leaned against the kitchen counter still dressed for court. He never loosened his tie or took off his jacket when buzzed.

At the stairs, I called up. "Kate! Molly! Time to eat!"

Now sixteen and twelve, Kate and Molly rumbled down the stairs, entering the kitchen. They had changed out of their school clothes into T-shirts and gym shorts. I could tell by their assessing gazes and distancing that they got his condition. I never discussed Gus's drinking with them; I acted as if I didn't notice, and all was normal.

"What's the matter, girls?" Gus said, spigoting himself a glass of water from the countertop pottery cooler. "You used to be glad to see me."

Both girls looked at him politely, stiffened slightly, and smiled back. Over the years they'd learned for themselves—and maybe by watching my double down on forced gay obliviousness—to sidestep confrontation when he was tanked. The ability to float like air was key, to make sure you came across as being as unthreatening as Cool Whip. It was heavy work to come off as so light a presence.

I plunked the salad bowl into the lineup of white enamel pots on the kitchen island. "Someone turn off the TV, please," I said. The news had drifted into *Entertainment Tonight*, which Kate zapped silent with the remote control. As per the experts, the TV stayed off at mealtime to optimize family bonding.

The girls served their plates from the countertop and slipped into the window-side of the table. The springy long plastic bench cushion sighed when they settled in.

"Don't eat until we're all ready." I dished my plate.

Gus took the *papacito* position at the end of the table. I sat down at his right. I was still in a ponytail, black Lycra, and Nikes from jogging before Molly's carpool.

"Say the blessing, Gus." I bowed my head and exhaled, pleased with how my family-meal moment was rolling out.

"Give us grateful hearts, our Father, for all thy mercies, and make us mindful of the needs of others. Amen."

We picked up our forks.

"I had Meals on Wheels today." To spark amiable table chatter, I had a mental list of table conversation starters that I'd stockpiled. "There's a wonderful man—Mr. Hayes. He's blind and lives in a pretty awful rooming house. He has the sweetest spirit of anyone on the route, though." I speared a mushroom. "You get that feeling being around him—that old soul, Dalai Lama kind of feel. There's something that's in the air about him."

Kate and Molly looked at me politely as they chewed. The forks clinked delicately.

I tried again. "Berry's checking if Mr. Hayes could get into the apartments at St. Mark's."

"Pass the salt," Gus said. A piece of lettuce, shiny with oil, had fallen off his fork, making a grease spot on his tan shirt. He didn't seem to notice it.

I handed the little glass salt cellar to him.

Kate forked a five-inch-wide clump of limp broccoli into her mouth. The ambitious size of her mouthful cut out any chance of a follow-up question about Mr. Hayes.

Gus looked at her as she munched. She caught his interest. A flash of parental authority and small frown seized him over the bulging broccoli cheeks. His shoulders straightened. "Don't you know how to eat?"

She downed the massive mouthful. "Huh?" Kate smiled and gazed around, looking everywhere but directly at Gus. Smart move. By looking up, but not into his eyes, she both acknowledged that she heard him yet sidestepped any hint of crossing him. Kate and Molly got that anything could potentially chap him when loaded. No matter how true or how funny the repartee you'd concocted inside your head, the right answer needed to be something patronizingly noncommittal.

His eyelids wrinkled into a squint at Kate. This wasn't exactly the conviviality that I'd wanted. "You heard me," he said.

A second after he spoke, however, his pique ebbed. He smiled to himself and then at her. "Where are you going to go to college?" he asked, jumping topics.

"I dunno." Kate dipped her fork back in her Gourmet Pasta Casserole serving.

The meal had just started. Maybe things would still turn around.

Gus's head tilted downward. His eyelids slackened until they almost shut. His head wobbled at shoulder height over his plate. It jerked a little as he started to lightly snooze.

Kate took a gulp from her water glass and hopped up. "I'm finished." The pink plaid bench cushion sighed when she rose.

Molly stood up with her own half-finished plate. "Me too." The girls' voices were carefully casual and good natured. They put their plates in the sink before heading upstairs to their rooms.

They must have silently thought the obvious, that I'd staged another supper in which they were to sit down and ad-lib normal with parental-lunatic bookends—Gus looping senseless, me wildly pretending not to notice or care. In hindsight, one thing is clear to me. When Molly and Kate hear talking heads cluck about how America has lost its bearings because the Family Supper is on the wane, I'm betting they won't necessarily buy in.

Gus's head bobbed up again at the sound of the girls scooting out of the window bench. Then he returned to the Gourmet Pasta Casserole in silence. I got nervous when solo with him drunk. He might or might not take a fast hostile turn, which he'd take furthest with me. He'd mess with my air space. A slammed door close by or fist bang on the table. He'd hurl something handy at the time like a copy of *Texas Monthly*. "You fucking bitch," he'd huff as it zipped by.

I haven't said this before, have I? Why haven't I? Because I didn't dwell on what I didn't think I could change without a breakup. I didn't want to leave the marriage, the life, the everything, it seemed, so I saved myself from acknowledging information that clearly wasn't great. I simply played as if things that happened didn't.

Example: Once I was eating a sloshy plate of spring English peas and onions at the kitchen island while he was pulling something out of the refrigerator a few feet away. I made a comment I thought was funny, but the feeling wasn't mutual. He lobbed the package of blue cheese in his hand my way. It skidded to a landing in my plate of soupy peas. The pea juice spattered all over me. Fight or flight? Neither. Instead I acted as if the previous minute never happened. Pea juice on my face, I straightened taller in my stool, lifted my chin, and put the next forkful in my mouth. The cheese package rose in the plate like a miniature saran-wrapped mountain. I looked straight ahead instead of at Gus beside me.

I don't mean to whine and double down as a victim. Mostly I just wanted Gus back as my partner. I missed him, the deep truth was. Instead, I found it easier to outwardly focus on denying his buzzed state or trying to proactively monitor him. That hurt less than admitting to myself how alone I'd come to feel. I couldn't change his liquid disappearances, so I tried not to even admit it.

Tonight at the table, he was within a solitary haze. He scraped up his last bits of hamburger and penne and pushed back his chair, leaving his empty plate. In the green chair, he snapped the television on. ESPN spread over the screen. He popped up the footrest and wiggled into his seat just so. He turned his face to the side, one cheek resting on the chair leather. He started snoring.

Our meal had lasted nine minutes.

I kept chewing my helping of Gourmet Pasta Casserole. My model family suppers were simpler once the others left. I could exhale and admire the ambience I'd cooked up. I helped myself to seconds of the ground beef with the fancy name.

Mardi Gras Party Menu: Sautéed Crawfish on Rice, Green Salad, Bananas Foster

At our annual Mardi Gras party, Eleanor and John Fontaine were side by side near the living room front window when I spotted them early on. They were hard to miss. John was in black tie. A rhinestone crown balanced on Eleanor's short gray hair. She waggled a glittery scepter. A cream satin cape flowed down her back. Their satin purple eye masks matched.

I wiggled through clumps of guests and sidestepped the coffee table to get to them. In age and in charisma, they were our oldest and grandest party guests. I knew Eleanor's food-festive MOW ways. She was carnival capable fashion-wise, too, I saw. In fact, she and John had lived at the French Quarter's core, the Pontalba Apartments on Jackson Square, at one point in their early life.

In a long-sleeved white tee, green sweater, black wool skirt, and a neck full of purple, green, and yellow parade throws, I was underdressed in comparison. The Fontaines outshined all the partygoers in the house, too—school parents, friends from church, and friends of Gus's and mine.

"You're spectacular, Eleanor," I said, gesturing at her finery.

"It's carnival." Eleanor had a no-nonsense tone as if having to remind me about gravity. She had to talk over Dr. John on the speakers. Behind her purple mask, her eyes were working the crowd with her usual intensity. Her mouth appeared amused.

"Well, this is a blast." Berry popped up beside the Fontaines and me out of nowhere.

"Berry!" I hugged him. His perky energy raised the volume on my own reservoir of baseline party perky. As I've pointed out before, to be a polite Mississippi woman—unless you have the earned gravitas of an Eleanor—you're compelled to crank out a sizeable share of enthusiasm at all times. It's just courteous. Berry's parade throws clinked against mine. "Hope you're having fun."

Someone else claimed the Fontaines to talk, and Berry and I stepped a few feet away.

"I almost didn't come," he said, looking around to see if anyone was listening. Little chance of that with Dr. John's loud growl rolling over the room.

Almost didn't come? Surprising, I thought, given Berry's puppy enthusiasm for a gathering. "Are you kidding? You had to come!"

"I know, but I've got a reason not to." His eyes ran another quick scan of the living room. "I quit drinking. Two weeks ago."

"Oh," I said. Oh is the go-to handy reply to cover pretty much any circumstance. You can leave it at that or use it as filler until you get a handle on a better response. It's the "whatever gets you through the night" of sticky conversation.

Berry didn't have a flirtini in his hand, I realized. Flirtinis were the house cocktail of the evening. I'd set out multiple glass pitchers full on the guest bedroom bar table along with six-dozen rented martini glasses.

"This is my first party since I quit," Berry said. "But how was I going to miss your party, though?"

"Glad you came! I'm honored you did," I told him. "And good for you for stopping drinking. That takes guts."

"I had to." He shrugged his shoulders and left it at that.

There was irony and cross-purpose in Berry's first sober night being my most booze-centric night of the year. The room sloshed with parents, friends, and parishioners and their flirtinis, sauvignon blanc, and Abita longnecks. The Neville Brothers now throbbed on the speakers. The irony was how Berry so matter-of-factly announced he'd quit. If Gus would do the same, it would solve all my problems, I thought. Recovery literature—not that I read it then—warns that it's delusion to think that once your loved one quits drinking, all your troubles will disappear. I would have been glad to test that truth out for myself, though.

True, I'd outwardly resolved not to dwell on Gus and my anxiety over him, but despite that, the subconscious part of my brain leaked panic that I might have to eventually do something in response. On morning jogs, the trance of my steps and the fresh air unleashed more than I intended. I involuntarily found myself praying inside my head for Gus to quit. Back home walking up the driveway, my system started the shift back to business as usual. I resolved to focus on all the good of Gus: his big heart, his humor, his smarts and love of family. All of it was true. By the time I was in the house, my resolve was back in business. Weren't Gus and I better off together than apart? I wanted the answer to be yes. Finding corroboration was my silent mission.

The carnival soirée in progress was part of my adaptation logic. After all, couples gravitate to occasions that fit them. The brainiac Perrys at our church hosted a thoughtful Lenten study on books by Desmond Tutu or Richard Rohr. The Cannons, Olympians of gardening, slated their annual Easter egg hunt and brunch for the peak of the hot-pink azaleas and neon beds of tulips. The well-mannered Halls had well-mannered Christmas cocktails with a soft-tinkling pianist and a dining table of silver chafing dishes. Gus and I were Mardi Gras naturals. Overdrinking and the resulting unleashed hijinks were carnival expectations. That meant I could cease my customary determined, exhausting merry oblivion to Gus's state for the event. I could take the party as it came. Being off the subconscious Gus case was a relief. That much I would halfway acknowledge to myself.

Time arrived to set out the night's main dish of sautéed crawfish on the dining table. Across the room, I saw Eleanor and John, heads huddling as they chuckled, flirtinis in hand. When Eleanor cocked her head John's way, her crown stayed put somehow. Berry was talking to our next-door neighbors Frank and John.

I spotted Gus through the French door glass on the porch off the living room. He was talking with some other St. Andrew's school parents. I could see his features in the porch light, the others in the circle leaning in, listening. Happiness lit up his face, and I don't just mean via Mondavi. There was connection, long-running friends, and satisfaction at how we'd pulled off one more carnival party for us and for them. The moment was one of those liminal flexes where time and self collapse into something briefly luminous: the experience of being at home yet having it filled with friends, New Orleans trumpets on the speakers, and the rite of our annual party coming off once more. I could adapt to what was. In terms of Gus and me, I could live in our life, what it was and would be. I felt it in my chest as the carnival beads clicked against my sweater. Everything would be okay, I told myself.

The night moved on. The purple tulips in vases started to wilt a tad as the party wound down.

Berry gave me a hug. "It's been great. I'm glad I did this."

"Love you, Berry. Hang in there." I raised my eyebrows as we locked pupils. He knew what I meant. I gave his arm an extra squeeze.

Gus spotted Berry leaving and crossed to the front door too. "Great to see you, buddy. Glad you could come." Gus put his hand on my shoulder. I put my palm on top of his proudly.

"Laissez le bon temps rouler," Berry said, his gaze sweeping Gus and staying there briefly. I knew what he was thinking and not saying, reading his own party-self past into Gus. Berry turned to me. "Two Thursdays from now's our day, right?"

"That's it."

"We can tell Mr. Hayes about the place at St. Mark's."

"Great there's a room. So much better than his place now."

Next morning, I collected the empty rental glasses. Seventeen of the six-dozen martini stems were gone. A few had hit the porch brick. A few others had walked off, I guessed. Seventeen missing martini glasses is a solid party war story, I thought. Those are some bragging rights.

As to the moment postparty when Gus rolled down the stairs and cracked a few ribs—and I couldn't have been more silently pleased he had—that part I just kept to myself.

MOW Menu: Barbecued Chicken, Stewed Okra, Baked Sweet Potatoes, Beaten Biscuits

It was 7:45 a.m. two days before Meals on Wheels. I spotted Tay's number when the phone rang. It was her son on the line, however.

"I'm so sorry about your father," I said. Word had spread that Tay's husband, Sherwood, had died the day before, after a downward health spiral at age ninety-two.

"Thank you," Joe said. "We're trying to make the funeral plans, and Mother won't do anything until she knows you've gotten her food. I've got two pans of barbecued chicken to bring you."

Chicken month. Good to know.

"Can I bring it now?" Joe asked.

"Of course. Please." First chicken delivery, then spouse's burial. Sherwood would have done the same if it were Tay's funeral to plan. In their sixty-five-year marriage, the two held St. Andrew's tightly. Any cause of the church was their cause.

Different skulls contain different points of view. Reminders of that truth kept rising up that day. Two stops into the ride, Berry's SUV turned onto Marion Dunbar Street toward our recipient Mrs. Shipp's house. The street was pretty run down, in my opinion. Maybe my wariness was merely that of an overreacting white delivery volunteer or maybe I was on target. In my opinion, Mrs. Shipp rivaled

Mr. Hayes for the worst combo of housing and street on our list. She shared her deteriorating yellow wood rental house with her teen grandson Tommy who appeared to have cognitive challenges. Berry tapped the brakes as we neared the Shipps' house. Five teenagers in matching red muscle shirts ran toward our car.

"Look at their clothes. That's cute," said Berry. "Wonder if they're in a dance troupe."

"Lock the doors," I said. Berry snapped the door locks.

They split into two clusters along both sides of the SUV. Two young men on my side and three on Berry's, peering in expressionlessly.

My eyes caught those of the guy closest to my glass. We stared blankly at each other, our noses about eighteen inches apart. He was maybe sixteen. What seemed like a surreal minute probably lasted less than that.

The guys didn't say anything, nor did we for that suspended moment.

I broke the silence. "Start inching forward," I said to Berry. "Go a tad so they have to move." The event seemed too surreal to think to panic.

Berry wormed forward. The guys took a few steps back. When his SUV cleared the group, I turned to look. The group was spanning the street still watching. I wasn't sure what the moment was about. I'm still not.

"What do we do about Mrs. Shipp's food?"

"I'm not stopping until the guys go away." I kept watching them in the rearview mirror, all still on the asphalt behind us. "Let's go to a few other houses and come back."

When we looped back forty-five minutes later, the teens weren't in sight. We never saw them again. Or maybe we did but didn't recognize them minus the red muscle shirts.

On our return to Mrs. Shipp's, she and Tommy were waiting for their meals. Mrs. Shipp, thin and barely five feet tall, wore a printed-scarf head wrap, duster, and slippers. Her lanky grandson Tommy stood up from the bare mattress in the living room corner where he always was when we arrived.

"Sorry we're running late." Berry handed one sack to her and the other to Tommy.

"That's all right," Mrs. Shipp said as we turned to go. "Y'all have a blessed day." I was pretty sure she didn't distinguish us from any of the other eight delivery teams from churches and Beth Israel temple, nor was there any reason she should.

Tommy nodded slightly. "Thanks." I'd never heard Tommy say anything before.

Now to Mr. Hayes's rooming house. Berry had found out from the St. Mark's Villa manager—Berry knew her through selling a house to her sister—that St. Mark's had a unit available for Mr. Hayes. Compared to his leaky, aging rooming house, the brightly lit seventies-era St. Mark's seemed like a slam dunk.

"I can't wait to tell him," said Berry.

On the porch with Mr. Hayes, Berry did.

"That sounds real nice, but I think I'll stay here," Mr. Hayes said. "I like it here."

We'd been inside his room. Its dingy cracked paint was ancient. The furniture consisted of a twin bed, a chest, and a wall calendar. There was an old boarded-up original fireplace, but the working heat source was a circa 1950 gas-burning ceramic space heater that pumped out as much in cloying fumes as it did warmth.

"It's pretty nice over there at St. Mark's, Mr. Hayes. Don't you want to go visit?" Berry asked. "We could run you over to look."

"Thank you, but I believe I'll just stay here." He offered the same upbeat appreciation for the St. Mark's footwork as he courteously showed for the lunches. "They treat me nice here, the other fellows. I'd hate to leave."

At Collins Dream Kitchen later, we mulled Mr. Hayes's reaction.

"Why would he want to stay there?" Berry asked. "St. Mark's is so much better."

"Let's try again next month," I said between forkfuls. "How's sober life?"

"Fine. I love my therapist. Do you know John Lever? He goes to St. Andrew's."

"I think I know his face. Doesn't he sit on the back-left side?"

"Uh-huh. Also, I like my gay AA group."

"That's great." I nodded. "I've always heard there's a noon AA group at St. Richard's that has four former Junior League presidents taking part. They all go out to lunch afterward. Pretty on brand. That's what club officers do no matter the group." I was starting to take note and file away what I overheard about AA and Al-Anon groups in town. I didn't want to go, though. That would be an admission of a problem. Despite the breakthrough-anxiety leaks in my head, I still tried to push dealing with Gus's drinking out of my mind. Better to not give it extra mental space.

"Are you okay?"

"Sure. Why?" I felt cornered as I lifted my glass of tea. Did I look nervous? I didn't think I did.

"You just seem stressed out. Like you're wound tight."

"Nope. Nothing new. Just life."

"John's great for me," Berry said, lifting a fork of catfish from his plate. "Think about going to see him sometime."

"Nah, I'm good." I concentrated on my plate as my fork chased down the remaining black-eyed peas.

"You're not fine, really," Berry said. "You're uptight." Then silence. Berry didn't say anymore. He took another bite.

None of us see things the same. That's a no-brainer yet sort of an earthshaker when you realize your read of what's happening is not necessarily anyone else's. Not Tay's, who balanced delivering her MOW barbecue chicken against her husband's loss. Not the Marion Dunbar Street guys' in red shirts, who regarded us in the SUV as Berry and I blinked right back. Not Mr. Hayes's, holding tight to his depressing room despite a spic-and-span unit with central heat available for him at St. Mark's. Not mine, blowing off Berry's questions over whether I was Fine Just Fine or not.

In the back of my head, there was a trapped, muffled thought that the stakes were rising, but I couldn't quite say in what way. Like the stare down with the red-muscle-shirt guys, I was locking eyes with what was in front of me and still couldn't say what I saw.

MOW Menu: Ham Slices with Jezebel Sauce, String Beans, Turnip Greens, Beaten Biscuits

"Ellen Ann? This is Tay. Are we meat or chicken this month?"

"Meat, Tay."

"That's right. I'll do ham."

"Wonderful. Maybe John could pick yours up and run it to me with Eleanor's bread."

"I'll call Eleanor and make sure."

"Thank you so much, Tay!"

"Thank you, Ellen Ann."

Tay and I had this same conversation on and off for most of the month now. MOW day was still three weeks off. It's said that with age, you become a more concentrated version of yourself. Tay's sense of MOW duty was intensifying, if that was even possible. She worried about missing the right day and whether it was the month for red meat or chicken.

On the eventual actual Thursday, John arrived with Eleanor's beaten biscuits and Tay's ham with Jezebel sauce. "We know Tay's calling you all the time," he said. "She calls us too."

"It shows how important this is to her," I said. "Those little tubs of Jezebel sauce as accompaniment. All the care she puts in."

"Eleanor and I are trying to get her to not fret over when's our day. The anxiety is taking over her mind. We tell her we'll remind her on time, and meanwhile relax. No need to fixate."

Afterward, John backed the Fontaines' old tan station wagon down the driveway. He veered into the front yard. A few mud ruts later, his station wagon finally made it out of the grass and down to the street. John had always navigated it without a thought until then.

On the route B delivery, Berry and I looked out for the guys in red shirts through the windshield. No sign of them as we approached Mrs. Shipp's.

"Um, look." Berry tilted his head at the yard coming up on the left. The red-shirt guys weren't there, but the Jackson Police SWAT team was. The navy-blue wagon with SWAT lettered on its side was on the left shoulder along with six or so other police cars. The SWAT team had multiple guns angled at a man lying on his stomach in the brown grass.

Did the scene have anything to do with the red-shirt guys? Or was it off track for me to think so? Was the man in the grass guilty? Of what? Or profiled? It was another month on Marion Dunbar Street and another load of data my head couldn't decipher.

Three doors past the SWAT scene, we parked at the Shipps'. Tommy Shipp came to the door.

"Thanks," Tommy said, taking both sacks. He didn't mention what was in progress down the street, nor did we. Tommy pulled out the tray with ham and Jezebel sauce and settled on the bare mattress in the living room. Mrs. Shipp called out "Thank you" from the back, out of sight. We closed the front door on the way out.

At his rooming house, Mr. Hayes waited on the porch.

"Beautiful day," he said.

"It is!" Mr. Hayes's positivity always spilled onto me. Part of being a southern woman is buying into a duty to think you have to take the lead role in pumping out cheerfulness in all interactions. As constitutionally upbeat as I was, Mr. Hayes's sunniness beat mine.

"Here you go," said Berry, handing over the sack. "Mr. Hayes, you sure you don't want to think about moving to St. Mark's? They've still got an apartment for you."

There was a flicker of tension in the muscles around Mr. Hayes's eyes. He was coming close to a frown at Berry. "No." He shook his head. "I appreciate the thought, but I'm going to stay here." His expression relaxed. "They treat me so good here. I wouldn't want to leave." The friction passed.

We had plenty to mull over lunch at Collins: the SWAT team and Mr. Hayes's second veto of St. Mark's.

"I can't believe he wouldn't want to go," I said between pork-chop bites. "And so he can stay there."

"I won't ask anymore. He's not interested." Berry looked around for a tea refill. The server, who'd been sitting at another table eating lunch, too, came over to top our jumbo glasses with unsweetened tea.

"You two doing okay today?" the man said.

"Just fine. How about you?" Berry replied.

"Fine. Let me know when you need something more."

Berry and he might have held eye contact a moment.

"Gaydar?" I said softly after the man left.

"I think."

Berry read people for sexual orientation in a sharper way than I ever did. With scant interaction, he'd note people in our Thursday routine who he thought were likely gay. The fact was neither here nor there, but it reminded me again of how different gazes pick up on different things. I, for one, could spot a likely problem drinker. I noticed a slightly puffy red nose and face. Often there was also this oversized general energy to them; I always loved that about them, in fact. I did in Gus.

Outside my wheelhouse, however, I missed a lot of the other human memos, I realized. I still didn't get the fine print on the red-muscle-shirt guys on Marion Dunbar Street. Or Mr. Hayes's apartment calculus. Or what the waiter and Berry knew with a quick pour from the tea pitcher.

Berry took a swallow. "Okay, what about you?" If Berry was going to let go of getting Mr. Hayes to St. Mark's, I was another story, it seemed. He was convinced I was brimming with anxiety. Was I? "How are you doing? Better than last month?"

"You're fixated on how I ought to go see John Lever, right?" I looked around for the tea guy. Maybe I needed some. "I'm fine." Did other people think I was coming apart too? Would they say so? Berry's probing unnerved me but I hoped I wasn't letting on.

"You know, you brought up Lever's name, not me," Berry took another bite of fried catfish. "Listen to you."

"I'm Fine Just Fine. I am."

"Well, you're not going to talk about it, it's clear," Berry said. "There's a heaviness to you now, you know."

I didn't buy what he was saying but didn't have a comeback. Nothing was different with me, I argued to myself. I could see where Berry thought he was due some candor reciprocity, though. He reeled off regular updates for me on his sexcapades, his own words. My head, however, had too much to lose to let myself veer off its paved path. "This banana pudding," I said to change the table temperature. "So good. I'm swooning."

Later at home before school pickup, I looked up John Lever's number. I didn't ask myself why. My index finger pushed call.

A few days later, when I sank into the nubby tan sofa at John Lever's office, I said, "I want you to know I'm Fine Just Fine."

"I'm delighted to hear that," John said in the armchair across the room.

Menu: None Because the Lowest-Cost Funeral Home Includes No Coffee or Pie

Mr. Hayes's body was in storage at the funeral home down the street from his rooming house. To those of us in Meals on Wheels, it was initially unclear how he'd died fourteen days earlier. Meanwhile, no relative had materialized to plan a service nor pay for one, according to the funeral home. The relatives hung up when contacted, the staff reported.

No money, no service, according to the funeral home. St. Andrew's offered to pay, but before actually doing so, the funeral home reversed course. There would be a service after all. The graveside service was set for 2 p.m. the next Saturday, cars to process together from the downtown facility to a plot at Autumn Woods cemetery for burial.

Meals on Wheels volunteers from St. Andrew's and the other half-dozen faith communities gathered for the service, the sole participants except for one extra arrival: a small German woman with frothy light-brown hair. She was a houseguest of a MOW volunteer from Beth Israel temple. She said she was in town to learn firsthand about the US South.

I asked her what she was discovering.

"I'd hate to say." She shook her head vigorously. Then she angled her face and fluffy hair in the other direction to cut off the conversation.

At the 2 p.m. service time, the funeral home possibly tried to gaslight us. The funeral director suddenly announced the service was off. "There remains a balance due," he said. He was middle aged with glasses and the expected somber suit and tie. "We won't proceed until the account is cleared." He was brisk about it. "Five hundred dollars."

First the surprise go-ahead for the service and now back to where we were—was bringing us there a bait and switch by the funeral home to suss out friends and family? We who made the effort to come were more likely to bankroll the arrangements than those who didn't bother. It was an astute maneuver, in fact. Yet not so fast, I thought. St. Andrew's would be willing to pay next week. Before any of us from the church could say so, the German visitor began to weep.

"None of you will pay? None of you?" The pain in her voice sharpened. She gasped and sobbed. No one said anything, both out of surprise and, honestly, because none of us did want to pay on the spot. We wanted St. Andrew's to. We'd come back for the service when the balance was settled. Maybe we'd move the service to St. Andrew's.

"I can't stand this!" Her grieving voice grew to a wail. "I'll pay!" She sobbed as the funeral director, with a professional blank face, sat down at his metal desk and ran her credit card for $500. Her tears were for the indignity done to Mr. Hayes, whom she'd never met, and also for how cold-hearted she thought we were. Nobody did comfort her or say anything to her, to tell the truth.

I wanted to think it was a misread of the moment. She bought Mr. Hayes a 2 p.m. funeral as scheduled, though. None of us who knew him did. It's possible we were all terrible.

Balance due paid, the director comprehensively switched to getting on with the service. The timbre of his voice dropped to rich stateliness. "The proceeding will now begin. Please follow our vehicles to Autumn Gardens cemetery for a graveside service on arrival." Partnering with the director was a broad-shouldered associate in

the requisite dark suit. They led in the gleaming black hearse. Two
other staffers followed in a somber four-door sedan, equally shiny.

Our caravan, headlights on, wound from downtown through
northwest Jackson, traffic pulling over in respect. We pulled into
Autumn Gardens, a bare, flat, treeless property near the city limits.

Interestingly, while the staff had bluffed briefly the day's service
was off, the grave site was ready for our arrival—well, Mr. Hayes's
arrival. The four funeral home representatives, spines erect, carried
the casket to the freshly dug plot with flawless dignity as our Meals
on Wheels delegation looked on.

The big-framed associate's voice boomed with pulpit-caliber reso-
nance. He recited from the Gospel of John: "You believe in God;
believe also in me. My Father's house has many rooms; if that were
not so, would I have told you that I am going there to prepare a
place for you?"

Ironic that in death, rooms were still the topic. It soothed my
conscience a little, smarting from the German woman's shade, that
Berry had futilely tried at least to prepare a room for Mr. Hayes at
St. Mark's.

The officiant's rich bass prayer rolled out over the flat Autumn
Woods grounds. I looked around at our multicongregational MOW
squad, most of us strangers to each other. The German woman continued to sniffle and glare at the rest of us with disgust.

"Amen," said the officiant. "The service is now concluded," he
added. One minute later, the funeral home staff vanished into their
vehicles to drive off without further discussion. Five hundred dollars
bought no extra margin of frills or time, apparently.

Unsurprisingly, the German woman didn't linger to talk with
the sorry likes of us. She left with her unnerved, sheepish host. Like
a surreal, appalled angel with a Visa, she'd come out of nowhere,
spontaneously paid for Mr. Hayes's service and then immediately
disappeared. The rest of us stayed graveside to try to piece together
what had happened to Mr. Hayes.

Our hearsay came from three different route volunteers who'd
arrived to try to deliver Mr. Hayes's lunches before MOW had

notification of his death. Different tenants told different MOW drivers what they knew.

"Mr. Hayes died of carbon monoxide in his bed," said the Presbyterian deliverer. "That's what one of the other tenants said. It was his space heater."

"One of the neighbors told me that some of the others at the rooming house scammed Mr. Hayes. They'd slip in his room—he wouldn't know they were inside—and steal his Social Security cash," said the Methodist.

"Mr. Hayes was afraid of doctors and hospitals. He wouldn't get that leg tumor checked out," said the St. Andrew's driver from the second Tuesday team. "Same with his eyes. He told me there was an operation for his sight, but he didn't want it. He was afraid and went blind because of it."

Mr. Hayes's trademark cheerfulness had always been extraordinary. Maybe the outer brightness that drew me to him was actually mere outer burn-off. Maybe the prime portion of his cheer stood as a firewall inside his own head. He chose to acknowledge what was beneficial to see and to not face the rest. His mental outlook had red lines, same as the outer, fixed tilt of his sightless face. He was careful about his vision in metaphorical ways, too, only seeing what he chose to.

Our Meals on Wheels lunches had been tiny temporary Band-Aids against his circumstances. Piecemeal meals. I portioned out my vision, too, of course, though I didn't get the parallel yet.

MOW Menu: Meat Loaf, Broccoli, Wild Rice, Beaten Biscuits

Now that Mr. Hayes was gone, Mrs. Shipp's living conditions were the shoddiest of anyone on the route. Her yellow rental had rotting clapboard with a few listless shrubs and a grassless, muddy yard. What's more, Marion Dunbar Street unnerved Berry and me due to the dramas with the SWAT team and the teens who crowded the

SUV. Berry checked with the St. Mark's administrator again. Yes, Mrs. Shipp could have an apartment, but not for Tommy too. St. Mark's was for seniors only.

"No, we'll keep together," Mrs. Shipp replied unsurprisingly. Caring for Tommy and life on her street seemed weighty for her tiny seventy-eight-year-old shoulders.

We never went back to Marion Dunbar Street, though. Before the following month's MOW Thursday, Mrs. Shipp was hospitalized and died. At the front of the chapel after her funeral service—arranged swiftly by her extended family at one of Jackson's most upscale funeral homes, not Mr. Hayes's—Berry and I met the great-niece who would be taking Tommy to her home.

He stood alongside the great-niece as we spoke. "I'm so sorry, Tommy," I said.

Tommy stared a moment, his eyelids cast down toward the beige carpet. "Thank you."

The grandniece's home was going to be different than Mrs. Shipp's. I guessed that based on her black suit, pearl lapel brooch, and friendly confidence. Even so, Tommy had lost a sturdy shelter with Mrs. Shipp's passing.

Turnover was happening fast with MOW, not only in terms of Mr. Hayes and Mrs. Shipp, but on the supply side too. John Fontaine could no longer back the tan station wagon down my driveway. To save his nerves and our grass, I started picking up Eleanor's bread from their house. The Fontaines made sure Tay's foil trays of meat or chicken were efficiently waiting for me at their house too. Soon after, however, Tay gave up her camellia-fronted house of fifty years for St. Catherine's Village. She would have kept on cooking ham and Jezebel sauce for the route if anyone at the retirement complex would have ferried her pans the ten miles south to my house.

New volunteer cooks replaced the old—women with daytime jobs. "I've been looking for a volunteer job I could do. This is perfect," noted one high school history teacher. "I can cook the night before. It takes an hour." I'd wake up on Thursday morning to a fleet of foil-wrapped pans of broccoli, wild rice, and meat loaf slices left on the kitchen porch before 8 a.m. The new volunteers operated with tight schedules and single, fast email swaps.

Change happened inside our house too. Kate departed for college. Molly entered ninth grade and joined a show choir. I'd drive her to weeknight practice and take a book to read until she was done. Supper was hit or miss on her practice nights. We'd come home to Gus snoozing in the green chair, his nightly condition the same.

After the next MOW delivery, Berry and I sat at Collins talking about the route B newcomers.

"Stan Jones is gay," Berry noted over fried catfish. Less than an hour before, the new recipient motioned us inside his small worn brown brick house.

"You kill me how you know that," I said. I didn't bring up my drinker-radar equivalency for puffy, rosy faces and a certain frequency wave of personal charm. I zero in on a person with oversized words, voice volume, and outlook. What stuck out to me wasn't that Stan Jones was straight or gay, but that there was a bottle of Old Crow on his kitchen counter at 11 a.m. How did that mix with the man's stroke rehab? He was fun, though. His sense of humor came through in his self-mocking pantomime of arm flaps and wry eye rolls to direct us in how to set out his lunch just so.

"Speaking of, gay AA is having the Christmas party at my house. You come." Berry fused the three rhyming syllables of the group name together into a three-beat package.

"Sure." I alternated between bites of the cabbage and the black-eyed peas on the day's plate. Nice that Berry included me in the party, but inviting me somewhat canceled the anonymous part of AA, I thought. The common denominator between me and Berry's group was John Lever, part of the AA group. I still went to him periodically. I'd sit on his sofa now and then to tell him how I was Fine Just Fine. We talked about boundaries and who and what got shares of my finite head space, including me. I always left with a snappier feel to my steps. John also insisted that I come to a Tuesday-night group session he ran, full of other women hashing out where they ended and their families began. In retrospect, it was strategic of

John to insist I go because I wouldn't have committed otherwise. It edged too close to mealtime at home. He ran the group along the lines of an Al-Anon meeting, but all kinds of boundary issues came into the conversation. I'd gotten to know the regulars and could talk a good game without ever getting to Gus and the drinking. I came away hoping I'd been entertaining during my turn. I assumed upbeat duty in group therapy, too.

"You're a friend of Bill's, huh?" Our Collins server held the tea pitcher over Berry's glass for a refill. He'd been listening from the table where he'd been sitting nearby.

"Sure am," Berry said.

"Me too," he said, pouring mine.

The server's remark surprised me. The world packed so much more than was on view in my ordinary sequence of school, grocery store, church, and mom-friend lunches. MOW stretched my middle-class, white, midlife, straight, married vision. Yet beyond nudging me wider on the city map, I also was touched by the map-free truth in the server's comment and Berry's easy reply: on any street, on any corner of town, humans were at work on inner tussles. There were ways to live and people who chose to dive below the everyday signals and expectations, no matter how accepted and shiny the outward looks. Thomas Merton warned against stopping at the surface, a gleaming one especially: "Be anything you like, be madmen, drunks, and bastards of every shape and form, but at all costs avoid one thing: being successful. . . . If you have learned only how to be a success, your life has probably been wasted." I give my years of Meals on Wheels credit for supplying a wider-angle view to me full of all kinds of people and all degrees of luster.

The Collins server sat back down at his solo table, resuming his own lunch plate of vegetables. Berry and I finished off the last tasty bites on our near-vacant plates.

My John Lever group was at 5 p.m. on Tuesdays. That was a dicey time of day logistically for me, but at least Molly's show choir didn't practice on Tuesdays. I'd rush home from the group by six thirty and get supper on the table. We each dropped a twenty-dollar bill in a basket in the center of our meeting circle for John while hearing the usual reports about family rubs and our own incorrigible drives to help others, to our own detriment as many times as not. That was the point frequently. Fixing others leaves only so much time for thinking too hard about yourself.

We went around the room as usual. My turn. I tried to not check my watch and worry about supper. Instead, I let myself notice that my mouth was opening. Words were coming out of it. "I'm wondering about my marriage. I might need to get out."

Group protocol prohibited feedback unless the person talking asked for it. I didn't. Instead, I went home and set the table. We ate. Gus snoozed in the recliner afterward. The clock ticked in every sense.

MOW Menu: Pork Tenderloin, Potato Casserole, String Beans, Beaten Biscuits

Of everything I hated about Gus's disappearance into the bottle, slinging this or that when he was drunk and angry was tops for me. It made it harder to deny trouble with actual physical objects sailing through the air. That nullified my determined work pretending all was tip-top. The next day he'd apologize and promise to hold both his temper and the projectiles next time. I wanted to believe him, so I did.

The next eruption occurred a few weeks after that last John Lever meeting. At home, a cardboard box full of desk supplies was sitting inside the front doorway. To punctuate his huff, Gus spotted the box, opened the front door, and hurled the carton out into the night. Pens, paper, and additional Office Depot whatnot sailed through the threshold and out into the azaleas and front yard grass. Drama itch scratched, and point made. Gus hazily returned to his green recliner.

I didn't realize an inner switch had flipped inside me. It must have, though. Either that or maybe it was the idea of a front yard display that nudged me somewhere new. In a symbolic and literal sense, Gus had thrown our stuff out into open air. I had nothing more to say specifically to him, though. I neither wanted to nor was there any point when he was foggy in the chair. I was more interested in cleaning the front yard. I robotically started the pickup, squatting for a Bic pen here, an aqua highlighter there. I was calm. That's when I noticed the shift in me. It was almost as if the new decision had physically plopped out of my body, like a passed kidney stone or a slippery newborn tumbling out into the world of oxygen.

The idea that had slipped out of me was visible and fascinating: I was done with marriage to Gus, in fact. I also noticed that I could handle this development without falling apart. I was ready to go into open air. A share of looking away from the possibility was self-protection. I dreaded what it would feel like to experience the moment when I admitted to myself that I was through. I'd be bringing fallout to all of us, a painful truth. I'd disconnected every time I came close to thinking about it for months. Maybe years.

What was the moment like when it happened? My skull and chest felt surreally calm, settled, and empty as I continued to pluck pads of pink Post-its from the oak leaves and a half dozen more Bics scattered around the palmettos. Back in the house, I peeked at Gus in his green chair, ESPN on the TV screen. I looked at his head and shoulders from the back. His posture was rigid, meaning he wasn't asleep. I said nothing and went to bed.

Gus was the one who asked me when we finally talked days later.

"So what's your problem?" he asked. "Do you want a divorce?"

"You know, I do," I said. "I've begged. I've cried. I've prayed. I'm done."

I'd crept toward the decision furtively, tentatively, and in denial as much as I could manage. Since that was the case, why would anyone think the divorce process wouldn't roll out in the same way? Gus wouldn't move out, nor did I see why I should, since I was a package deal with Molly, Sonny, and Molasses. Gus and I continued to live at home, have supper together, and from time to time have sex. We teamed up to go to church and a few Christmas parties, unnerving

and confusing everyone. I'd spent my entire life being nice and man-
nerly. I didn't know how to act otherwise when the agenda was
busting up a twenty-three-year marriage and a household.

But acting nice didn't mean, out of eyeshot, I didn't have a to-do
list. I went to the bank and pulled out a stack of cash from an extra
account we'd set aside to pay quarterly taxes. I drove around the
corner to a different bank and opened an account in my own name.
When the pad of fresh new blue checks arrived, I made out the first
one for Berry's, well, my lawyer's retainer fee.

Week by week, Mrs. Sanders witnessed our one-roof, one-
divorce-in-progress living setup. My move to the downstairs guest
room produced yet a fourth set of sheets to wash. She didn't comment on the estrangement, however, nor allow herself to display any
reaction at all to the news. She was nonjudgmental, the in-house
Switzerland on Tuesday and Thursday workdays.

Due to the showy sanctimony of the Mississippi Legislature, the
state is one of the nation's hardest for obtaining a no-fault divorce.
Both parties have to agree on absolutely everything to manage one.
The catch-22, of course, is that if you two agreed on absolutely everything, you wouldn't divorce in the first place.

I wanted Gus to sign the papers. He was firm on two points: (1) not
wanting to sign the papers and (2) not changing his drinking habits.

"You promised to love me for better or for worse," he said.

"Which doesn't mean you can do any old thing, and it's my job
to deal with it," I said.

A window unpredictably opened in the stonewalling, however.
A couple with two little boys made a solid offer on the house before
we had time to put it up for sale. Berry navigated the contract, naturally. The buyers offered to delay closing until school was out, two
months ahead. Gus was willing to sign the house offer but still not
the divorce papers. The weeks passed. Gus went to work and came
home as if nothing was different. I can see why he thought he could
keep as-iffing our life, since I rolled along right there, still in the
house too. I stuck to my old routine, including Meals on Wheels.

Midmorning one MOW Thursday, I had the foam trays lined up on the island. I was spooning potato and cheese casserole into one of the upper compartments in the eighteen open trays. The microwave hummed, a Pyrex of string beans reheating.

Gus appeared in the kitchen, headed out the door to work. From the purposeful tap of his steps in his lace-up dress shoes, he was all business and sober. "I need you to check on some payments," he said.

"I can't stop now. The Meals on Wheels drivers are nearly here."

"No, I need it now. I've got an eleven o'clock," he said.

"I've got an eleven o'clock too." Berry and Frances Jean would be driving up for the meals then. I felt the familiar sense of being caught trying to balance out between Gus and the rest of existence.

"This is important," he said.

"So's this."

The point hit me. Exactly why was I ladling potatoes solo as Gus looked on? Wasn't I performing the typecasting that I howled about, the expectation that projects like MOW are dumped on over-forty women? And in our own marital case, of how I thought Gus had ducked out emotionally as a partner, along with leaving me to deal with the entire logistical family and life bag?

"You're just standing here," I said, mid–potato casserole. "If you want me to look up the payments, help finish this. Get a spoon." I was telling myself this as much as I was telling it to Gus and to the listening ears of life in general. "Here." I stuck a black plastic slotted serving spoon in his direction. In his starched white shirt and blue tie, he looked startled and confused. He took it.

It was as if we'd hit reboot. He put his stack of legal files on the stool by the island. To my surprise, he silently and conscientiously started ladling the creamy, drippy potatoes into the tray compartments.

Mrs. Sanders passed through the kitchen with dirty sheets. Behind her big pink-framed glasses, her eyes were taking in the sight of Gus systematically filling all the trays on his side of the countertop. She said nothing.

I started shoveling the string beans into the remaining Styrofoam compartments. Gus slipped his tie into the button placket of his white shirt to protect it from grease. He continued working his way down the counter, tray by tray.

I wish I could say that this Thursday potato moment brought us together, that over a cheese-topped casserole, string beans, and the rhythmic motions of our synchronized slotted serving spoons, we found a mutual hunger to make things right. The truth is we just filled the trays in silence. It needed to happen, and so it did. Afterward, I found the bank deposit information he wanted. He backed down the driveway for his office. The route drivers arrived.

Maybe something did shift, however. Not long after that, Gus signed the no-fault divorce papers alongside me in a branch bank in his office building, a bank we'd never previously entered nor would ever enter again. The secretary was a notary, though, which is what we needed for the signatures to be legal.

Back home in the kitchen after the signing, I wrapped my arms around Gus's waist, and he pulled me to him around the shoulders. We latched onto each other for a long while, or it seemed so to me. I felt the punch of what had occurred. I felt broken in two, specifically. Judging from the shakes of his shoulders along with my own as we sobbed, I think he felt the same. He pulled his wide gold wedding band off and gave it to me to keep. "I'll always wear it," I sniffed. That's what a widowed friend of mine did with her dead husband's. In that moment, I was sure I would. I loved Gus but couldn't live any longer under the same terms or roof. And let's be honest, given the choice of me or drink, he didn't choose me. It was time to face that. I think coming to acknowledge that choice of his was what terrified me as much as the logistics of divorce.

What was the lesson of Meals on Wheels? How did my seventeen years of second Thursdays overlap with the rest of my life? For one, looking back, I see that I came across situations bigger than I or any other sole person could solve in the lives of Mr. Hayes, Mrs. Shipp and Tommy, and, of course, Gus and me.

Life happened, and so did Meals on Wheels, month by month. Through Mr. Hayes, Mrs. Shipp, Tommy, and Tayleanor, MOW was a microcosm of what being human meant in Jackson, Mississippi, in assorted shoes. It also spoke to change's certainty and time's onward slog. Not that I saw all that then, but it was there.

Here's something else. In retrospect, I see all the curious forces of unexpected, unlikely support that were serendipitously present in the rough parts. Secret angels, if you will. I didn't like the weeping, accusatory wavy-haired German visitor at the funeral home at Mr. Hayes's death. Yet she came out of nowhere, paid for Mr. Hayes's funeral on her Visa and huffed off, never seen again. No one said an angel can't be surly.

If the German was a mystical come-and-go snarler, Berry's support was the opposite. He was a constant route B and Collins Dream Kitchen friend—I count possibly 156 fried-catfish and pork-chop lunches we shared. You've got to talk about something, as he noted of working in real estate. Over all the Thursdays, he listened to what I didn't say as much what I airily did. Pork chop by pork chop, the right names opportunely popped out of his mouth. His shrink and his divorce lawyer became mine. Naturally, Berry was my real estate agent when I moved to a new smaller ranch house near his. He was crucial in the switch points on my way. He worried whether he was enough of a networker for Jackson real estate. All I know is that he was my junction signal at spot after spot.

Eventually the dust started to settle. About that time, I ran into Molly MacWade, the priest who'd sweetly cornered me into volunteering for Meals on Wheels years before. With on-brand cheer, I reported to her that my new house has a shiny, longish counter that worked for MOW too.

"Meals on Wheels? No way," she said, a chuckle slipping out. "You're still doing that? How long does that make?" She stepped along, laughing and shaking her head.

Chapter 13

Safely above the New Orleans Parade

I AM WRITING THIS IN AN 1832 BRICK HOUSE ON JULIA STREET IN New Orleans, a place with all the mildew, mortar dust, and karma you'd imagine a New Orleans building would have. I write, but don't live, here—if living means more than a MacBook, a tomato sandwich, and a passable amount of upkeep for my two rooms and myself. For part of each week, I leave my two daughters and my home in Jackson, Mississippi, 192 miles away, to coop myself up in a place famous for its live-music venues and restaurants.

Why?

One reason is that I have gone to New Orleans for years. My ex-husband felt its draw, too, and early on we rented a garage apartment near Audubon Park. The city became a component of our marriage and of our daughters' childhoods. And so, when my marriage ended and my ex held on to our place, I wanted, in an act of self-expansion, to have a pied-à-terre of my own.

It's very Mississippi of me, really, the draw to the city. New Orleans has always seduced upstate Mississippians who've come here to blow off steam for generations. It's the antidote to Mississippi's granular prissiness that comes out of Protestant churchy stiffness. For me, brought up Baptist, it only took one family stroll around the Quarter at age five to see that the rules of sanctioned Mississippi propriety didn't apply here. All dessert, all the time was the mojo of the stripe-canopied Café Du Monde, the outdoor terrace of tables where people heedlessly wolfed down plate-loads of powdered sugar beignets—no precursor meal or green vegetables necessary. What's more, through Bourbon Street bar doorways, I spied bored dancers in spangled pasties on countertops, blankly grinding to whatever came through the loudspeaker. For a tender Baptist from the Delta, nipple tassels and dessert-first were confirmation that a wider world existed. My consciousness ignited, humming like the engines of a parking lot full of church buses.

New Orleans is the key to a Mississippian's locked-up longing, a meetup doable with a half tank of gas and three hours for a ride south on I-55. To be honest, the boost of New Orleans may not be all due to the town's looser particulars. Some of New Orleans's attraction is just that it's not small-pond Mississippi. You can get lost in a way impossible at home, a heady mindset in itself. Gus felt the New Orleans draw, too, and courted business here to increase the reasons to visit. (Looking back, what a dutiful Mississippi Protestant work ethic rationale to use.)

As much as I loved the city, small doses were fine. For years, my low threshold came through at Mardi Gras. Our family always seemed to end up wedged along the St. Charles parade route with deceptively harmless-looking partyers in their late teens, most likely in college. They'd look normal enough in their parade gear of jeans, sunglasses, and starter swags of beads around their necks. Inevitably I'd realize they were hell-bent on creating an epic lost-weekend memory as I stood alongside. I'd stop them from sizzling us with the cigarettes in their frantic, flapping hands and from stamping Molly's and Kate's knuckles as they lurched in delirious happiness to poach bead strings from our patch of the pavement. After a mere hour or so, I'd have my fill for the year.

Gus loved carnival and celebrated parade days through a predictable string of nuclear-grade Bloody Marys. Our biggest fight ever was after three back-to-back Saturday parades when we clashed over how his vodka rite left me to parent solo. In some ways secretly I don't think I ever moved on from that dispute for the duration of our marriage. We repeated the fight a lot, in New Orleans and in Mississippi, Mardi Gras or not. Over the years, my argument widened from how his intake left me as the solo parent at Mardi Gras to eventually how he simply, in effect, left me solo altogether. Maybe I never could shed my share of tut-tutting Mississippi church-lady DNA, an outlook that sunk our marriage as much as the vodka. Who's to say?

When a marriage ends in midlife, some women go looking for a stubbled, kicked-back man boy, others are forced into retail, to ring up Tory Burch flats for women—probably married stay-at-homes—who can afford them. As for me, once the dust settled and I blocked out a first-of-the-week teaching schedule, I decided I wanted my own part-time New Orleans quarters. Gus had kept our old one. A complete move to New Orleans wasn't my plan. Molly and Kate weren't quite grown, and I had my Jackson job, friends, and house that I liked. I assumed I'd be giving myself a city base, a place to go, take a bath, and head back out the door in search of oysters or a parade—a short tame procession would be fine for me.

My apartment is near Lafayette Square, in a row of thirteen Federal town houses known as the Sisters of Julia Street that were built outside the French Quarter after the Louisiana Purchase. This neighborhood was the original Uptown (Henry Clay's daughter lived here), but it also had a skid row era that lasted from the mid-1900s until its restoration and gentrification began in the 1980s.

My rooms are in the first town house to be restored, in 1981, so the renewal itself was dated when I moved in. It was a mix of powdery pre–Civil War mortar and 1980s cabinets and white ceiling tiles. There was an obviousness to this restoration, and I liked that. I was restoring myself, too, wasn't I?

I couldn't afford the apartment, but I decided to take it and deal with that problem later. And so, in February 2008, I watched myself write out a pale-blue check for the first month's rent.

Soon I was taking a stool at Felix's oyster bar counter and getting a table for one at Herbsaint. I took myself to Tipitina's and d.b.a. where I would sip club soda by myself and mildly and happily nod along with the set. The rowdier the other patrons, the more I unnerved them. Upbeat drunks edged away from me, fearful that a loner like me had to be a shooter. I noticed anxiety in people's eyes as they sidled away, no matter if it was at a city Christmas carol sing in Jackson Square or an Ani DiFranco show at the House of Blues. It was probably inevitable that all those tables for one for me would eventually grow stale.

Apart from long-standing habit, I also rent this apartment because I am a writer, and I write better in New Orleans than I do elsewhere.

Why? No one I love is here, and no one here cares anything much about me. I'm not opposed to loved ones, but their absence makes working simple. At home, I collaborate against myself: I end up telephoning the pharmacy for my college-age daughter, who is capable of handling it herself, or I think about a student's writing when I should be thinking about my own. I believe the Mississippi Symphony can't proceed without me in the audience at its Saturday-night concerts.

Measured by my writing, there's no doubt my New Orleans solitude works. When I was finishing a master's degree, and my thesis deadline loomed, the page count mounted much faster on Julia Street than in Jackson. In my first productive hot streak here, I wrote from morning until bedtime for five days straight. I left the building only to run.

Here's my voyeur ritual on my daily riverside run through Woldenberg Park: I spy on the sax player—not that I've ever spoken to him—who stakes out the day's tourists. Perched on his regular bench, his tip box beside his shoes on the sidewalk, the guy keeps a lookout for a prospective target: a vacationing family. "Hey! Kids!" he opens with the brightness of a TV host. There's a trademark one-second pause in how he throws out the two-word come-on. I wait for the tiny pause in his pitch, and it always comes. The family returns his smile, and—I've run past by now, but I'm still listening behind me as I lope forward—he starts puffing out the Sesame Street theme for a thousandth round. There is not one other song in his repertoire. I like his MO, however. My life here runs on minimalism too. Just because a routine's simple doesn't mean it's not right.

I swapped street brushups for real human companionship. My silent apartment is a counterweight to the instant gratification of eavesdropping street dialogues and the energy of Saints home game weekends. To get a human fix, I just go outside. It's the counter-intuitive truth that a rowdy place like New Orleans complements solitary living.

This doesn't mean I don't need the surrounding city. Far from it. I feel a vital energy moving through me when my Ford enters the tree tunnel of South Carrollton Avenue, lined with palm-fronted, two-story homes. Even more than the city's manicured look, however, I love its careless beauty: the gingerbread trim on a decrepit Queen Anne, say, that has been hacked into apartments for piercing- and juice-shop types.

But for a New Orleans obsessive, I'm easily satisfied. I need the city's exuberance, but only in careful doses.

As a confirmed onlooker, I have the same urge that motivates all secondhand breathers of life. I want to stay on the sidelines. I crave distance between the parade and myself, both the actual processions in New Orleans (parades go by all the time) and the steady lineup of disruptions at home because of a teaching schedule, two young-adult daughters, and a tense eight-pound dog.

In splitting my life between Jackson and New Orleans, I've apportioned myself, both geographically and metaphorically, between two "states": one home for family and society, another for solitude.

More than eight decades ago, Virginia Woolf said that for a woman to write, she needs a room of her own, her symbol for physical space, money, and freedom from interruption. Culture is not the only reason such a room eludes women's grasp; their instinct to please and be available to others also plays a role.

It is no coincidence that as aspiring writers, William Faulkner and Tennessee Williams moved to New Orleans to write for a season, but their fellow Mississippi author Eudora Welty did not. Welty remained in Jackson and took care of her high-maintenance elderly mother, which cost her years of writing time. It was Faulkner who famously said, "If a writer has to rob his mother, he will not hesitate. The 'Ode on a Grecian Urn' is worth any number of old ladies." It was also Faulkner who wrote *Soldiers' Pay*, his first novel, in a Quarter apartment on Pirate's Alley.

Maybe my apartment is less an exercise in Oprah-like self-expansion than a real-time demonstration of how my overdutiful-ness cuts into my productivity, too near family and friends. It doesn't speak well of my support of my own ambition to only stumble onto the discovery of what the apartment does for me as a productive writer.

Of course, I'm not the first woman (or man) to rethink at midlife. Time, jobs, and children move along. It's healthy and so fifty-five-ish of me to make a move to resist and revise. That is a kinder way to see myself than as a writer still on the periphery, typing with per-sistence, but with no contract for an important book (or any book at all, for that matter).

Still, I realize that I backed into claiming a room of my own. Handing over that first rent check, I assumed I was giving myself a base for spending time in New Orleans, a place to go, take a bath, and then head back out the door in search of oysters or this week's parade. But my Julia Street apartment is more about what happens inside my own head.

Fellow New Orleans lovers in Jackson sometimes ask me to alert them to apartment vacancies so they can rent a place in the city, too. I cheerfully say I will. But I won't. I don't want to start texting them supper invitations to join me at Julia Street or start half-hoping that they will stand under the fanlight window at my front door and buzz my apartment. And Virginia Woolf knows that, given half a chance, I would.

Chapter 14

The Weight of Cinders

THE EARTH'S MANTLE IS INEVITABLY CREEPING. IT'S NOT NOTICE-
able until it is, tectonically speaking. My daughter Molly's boyfriend,
Jack, made the call to me from New Orleans around 6 p.m. Thursday.
Molly couldn't.

"He's gone." There was a crack in Jack's voice between the seismic
sounds of the first and second syllable.

Here's what happened, Jack said: Molly had driven over to Gus's
after work. She found Gus napping in bed—in our old barge of a
carved mahogany-reproduction king that Gus had moved to New
Orleans postdivorce—dressed in his khakis and squeezing a pillow sideways, his go-to sleep position. She gave him a noogie. He
was cool—dead, actually. Molly froze bedside until Jack could work
through thirty minutes' worth of afternoon traffic to the Marigny.
Despite my perpetual predictions that his drinking was going to
cause a car wreck or cracked skull, Gus died from a heart attack or
stroke in his sleep, the coroner pronounced. Atherosclerotic cardio-
vascular disease, officially, leading to what looked like a peaceful,
instant death on our old mattress.

What had been our story had just turned into my story to take
forward. I was going to be the sole archive and depository of our
shared past. For some reason, that was how Gus's death sank in for
me. It felt cause for panic. Despite having had almost no conversation in a year or so, his departure hit me hard. Being the only one
on earth who remembered so many particulars made me feel alone
in an existential way. Did it mean less if no one on earth remembered but me? It might, I suspected. I was not just confronting the

prospect of the death of memories of the marriage, but also the death of big chunks of me, clearly. I was the sole container left of lots of history that made up prime meaning in my life. This was a form of loss that had never occurred to me before. Along with being stunned, I was also intrigued by my alarm. I hadn't known this was something to fear.

Many humans have some kind of midlife mortality epiphany. It turned out that Gus's death was mine. In the end, it's always about ourselves. Of course, I mean me in this case. I wanted our marriage to have mattered. What's more, being left as the custodian of that history felt like one more way for Gus to leave me feeling alone. In the marriage I felt emotionally abandoned to his drinking fog. Now I felt I'd been left solo to care for decades of memories. The idea seemed like a version of the old puzzle of whether there's a sound in the forest if no one's there to hear it. There was no other skull on earth that matched the set of marital and family history inside my own, data that mattered.

I stuffed a suitcase for the three-hour I-55 drive through the two-state stretch of pine trees, gas stations, roadside drive-throughs, and the final swab of south Louisiana wetlands outside of the city.

At Schoen Funeral Home, a 1920s buff stucco Mediterranean mansion on Canal Street, Molly and Kate robotically made arrangements—what a hands-off euphemism of a word to sidestep what's going on. First there'd be a service at a tiny Episcopal church nearby, including the Storyville Stompers brass band, followed by jambalaya for all at Gus's house. Gus loved Episcopal pomp. It's unsurprising, actually, that a guy with big thirst and big angst would go in for big liturgy featuring bells, incense, and bobbing processional banners. Gus liked everything big. Even sweeter, the church of choice was known for welcoming dogs to services, which indicated it wasn't the stuffiest place.

As an ex, I had a thin line to walk, even as I obsessed over my keeper-of-the-memories epiphany. I made a therapy appointment to vent for an hour. Outwardly, I wanted to be on hand for Kate and Molly but stay at the edge. In the last years, Kate and Molly had lived out the truism that it's the children who get custody of divorcing parents, not vice versa. They'd done a share of caretaking bruised parents in ways that children in intact families aren't called upon to do. As for Gus, he'd had good and bad periods since the divorce. Yet his business always thrived. He'd always insisted drinking came with the legal culture and pressure, and he'd be a package deal. We all are at our cores, of course.

Good taste demanded I wedge into the right spot memorial-wise: I should be present but at the periphery. This was the South, and there was an unspoken etiquette to the particulars, no different than other public moments involving punier stakes. Making too big a display of yourself at your ex's funeral was tacky and theatrical.

I grieved Gus's death, along with its message that mortality was edging closer to me as well. Learning that—I mean how my insides pounded, and I burst open waterwise—was a surprise to me. For one, I hadn't counted on the heartbreak of seeing Kate's and Molly's heartbreak. Losing a parent is supposed to be later along in the arc of adulthood than this. Witnessing Kate and Molly having to deal with a father's death in young adulthood, hovering in their late twenties, was akin to having to watch them as toddlers run and inevitably bloody their heads in the process. Most people lose parents, but not before their adult life has gotten off the ground. Kate and Molly were facing the truth that comes sooner or later to breathing humans: love eventually is going to leave you holding the bag. It's the cost of it. I ached for their aching in a way that I might have missed if I'd been an official grieving spouse.

I looked at the photos on the chest in Gus's Marigny living room of family trips and one of us two on a cruise two years before the split. I was surprised he had the photo out on display. "If we hadn't divorced, he wouldn't be dead, I think." I snuffled. "But I couldn't stay."

"You don't have to think that, Mom," both daughters murmured.

I did think about it, of course. Yet just as importantly, a share of my tears flowed, I suspect, simply because I wanted to mourn alongside Kate and Molly. It felt like a way to prove ourselves still a fused family, despite the divorce and death. There's primal power and need in responding in pack fashion, like breathing in unison or having your periods eventually synchronize when you share a roof. To cry with Kate and Molly over Gus was reassuring. It felt like a measure of reprieve to me for imploding their lives with the divorce.

Gus's death brought out another fact. Although the years had ticked by since the dissolution, Gus remained the organizing principle of my life, even though we'd hardly been speaking. My postdivorce chapter as a French teacher and uptick in my journalism gigs were alternatives to how I'd assumed life would play out with Gus. I'd imagined a lifetime of more of the same: doing his business bookkeeping; going to lunch with my empty-nest mom pals and turning out the occasional local magazine piece when the spirit moved me. Also continuing would be my suppressed dissatisfactions and policing of his drinking too. We'd talked about retiring on C-30 A in Walton County, Florida, our favorite stretch of Gulf beach.

The truth was that I liked my present plan B life fine. Yet that doesn't mean it wasn't plan B. I'd wanted Gus to toe the line and for us to be together.

Is this where I'm supposed to say everything worked out for the best? I can't. What I wanted was what I'd originally picked: my version of Gus who would want to quit drinking so my idea of life resumed. If you can dream it, you can be it, pop culture promises. I could dream it, for what that's worth. No dice, though. Gus's death brought up the bleed-out again, the failure rising up in my head like a corpse that pushes its way out of the ground in a flood.

In Jenny Boully's essay "The *Future Imagined*, the *Past Imagined*," she writes, "And nothing is as confusing, as cryptic, as encoded as what occurs, as what is said, when we leave a love affair and suddenly have to live again outside of dream." As long as the dream looms, "something *could occur, might occur, should occur, would occur, could have occurred, might have occurred, should have occurred, or would have occurred.*" Time was up.

At the right moment—and Gus's death was it—I was perfectly happy to beat myself up over being the one to end the marriage. I could temporarily ignore how the marriage had ended when I gave up on the idea that there'd ever be more than an outer shell left of it due to the vodka creep. Yet now an aftershock of guilt was my way of honoring our past. I was showing up, and I was sorrowful. Women are trained to be good at that.

What women also do is oversee funerals. This funeral story comes with a particular curveball that began at bedtime three days before the Saturday of Gus's service. On TV as I adjusted the blanket on the bed, I noted that CNN was saying there was a developing Gulf storm worth watching. Next day I called the church concerned about what we'd do if the hurricane headed toward New Orleans. The church administrator blew off my anxiety. "Don't you worry. We're pros. This is New Orleans. We're on," he said. "If the storm really comes, the weather won't get here till late Saturday night."

The storm's name, you ask? I kid you not: it was to be Hurricane Gus.

And so on Saturday morning, I was driving to Gus's house, two miles to go. I was squeezed in my black funeral skirt, clean white blouse, and black patent flats. I answered the phone as I steered. It was the priest. "Look, we're going to have to reschedule," he said.

My voice squeaked back as I chugged toward the Marigny. "It's too late to cancel. Everyone's here." They were. One of Gus's friends had flown in from California, hurricane be damned. Others were heading into town at that moment, driving in from Jackson and Mobile on gusty interstates for Gus.

The priest either didn't listen or didn't care. Both, I'm pretty sure, when I think back. "Well, tell them it's off," he ordered. "Do a telephone chain." All that clerical bravado of thirty-six hours before had vaporized. That was it.

I never heard another word from the guy. (Kate's radar on him had gone off when we'd gone to the previous week's Sunday service to get a sense of the church's feel. She'd eyed an edict in the bulletin that declared that Communion was for baptized Christians only. In fairness, maybe the directive was to keep dog owners from feeding Communion wafers to pets, or maybe it hinted at, oh, the kind of hard-line, legalistic collared ass who'd bail on a family's funeral two hours before.)

We regrouped. Gus wouldn't have wanted a priest who was a dick in charge anyway. A free-form funeral with no church support it was to be, thank you. First, Kate's fast-thinking in-laws pulled our waiting white lilies off the church altar in the wake of the cancellation, since the church was still open. Jack printed Office Depot service bulletins from the PDF the church had sent us to proof two days before. At least the Storyville Stompers, more empathetic and conscientious than the priest, reconfirmed that they'd take part, no matter.

The Weather Channel announcer speculated on where Hurricane Gus would hit, anywhere from Florida to Louisiana. There was no rain so far, but the day was gray and cloudy. Outside Gus's house, wind whipped down Dauphine Street. We turned off the television. The Weather Channel is structured to pump out anxiety to keep you tuned in, the cable TV version of the standard bar trick of feeding customers too-salty peanuts so you stay thirsty.

Arrivals began filling Gus's nineteenth-century shotgun double. The original interior walls had been knocked out to create one big space, the bomb for a big funeral service, actually. The white lilies, jambalaya, salad, and banana pudding stood ready on the counter. Outside the glass-paned Victorian front door, the Storyville Stompers knocked and looked in. All in regulation black pants, white shirts, black ties, and gold-braided caps, they squeezed through the doorway along with a tuba and marching bass drum. The trombonist took one side of the room, the four other musicians the opposite wall below the stair rail to upstairs. Some were middle-aged Black men, some white.

"Lord, Lord, Lord, you sure been good to me," the strawberry-blond, gravel-voiced trumpeter began to croon. Brass, cymbals, and drum thwaps spilled out across the downstairs, the rooms full of the smell of the jambalaya and lilies. "Lord You Sure Been Good to Me" has been the opener for New Orleans brass band funeral programs since the heyday of the Olympia Band. The roomy directive in the song's message makes it a particularly good start, almost cajoling listeners to gratitude over the good that had been shared with the honoree. Or maybe that's just how the song seemed to me since that's how I felt.

I burst into tears. Sure, I was caught up in a measure of rosy remembering—Gus had, after all, selected alcohol over me—and what family doesn't idealize their departed—yet there was movement inside me of my own making too. Gus's death unlocked a gate that had needed to stay shut if I were going to come to grips with the marriage's end and move on. Any conscious, careful breeziness in the aftermath on my part had been my essential wind tunnel for me to reboot. Gus's death concluded the need for all that determined chipperness. All matters Gus roared into ditches inside me walled off until now.

"The Old Rugged Cross." "I'll Fly Away." "When You're Smiling." "You Are My Sunshine." "Iko Iko."

The Storyville Stompers took turns rotating solos on horn, drum, and vocals. From godly to playful to febrile and rowdy, back to the bedrock of connection, to what it means to find people to love. The songs wagged truth, familiar and fundamental to my ears.

Life isn't as ordered as a jazz playlist at a funeral, yet there'd been happiness in the imperfect march of Gus and me. The qualities that drew me to Gus were the flip side of what came to be deal breakers. Gus was big and fragile and damaged and often wonderful. The holes in me matched the corresponding waiting places in him. That truth and the band pounded in my ears.

"I'll never let you down," Gus used to say, and we both knew the words were what we each wanted to hear. He loved me best he could. I did the same for him.

It's true I was curating my memories. We'd had neither the worst divorce in the world nor the best. Midrange in acrimony and emotional abuse, I'd rate it. Memory shaping was what remained for the story of Gus and me, same as it is for all remaining partners. I remained blown away that I was the one—the sole person on earth—to bear witness to our full story, the good and bad. It was true that Gus left me liquidly, and I left him in real time. Yet I was remembering and momentarily delighted, tuba oompahs shaking my chest. Me holding love's bag.

A caricature of Gus's face, with round glasses and trim beard, smiled up from the stack of printed white handkerchiefs. Kate's art-teacher husband, Scott, had drawn the likeness. Handkerchiefs, customized via Etsy, are staples of a New Orleans funeral. A few songs into the Stompers program, our poised Mississippi friend Martha did the proper thing in plucking the top handkerchief off the stack and beginning a second line. Everyone fell in behind Martha, her multiple opera-length pearl strings flapping. "When the Saints" rose to the ceiling. We waved Gus handkerchiefs and snaked through Gus's house. After a stanza or so, I stepped out and resumed my seat on the ice chest in the hall, a pretty metaphorically apt spot for an ex. As guests swayed along, it was as if I was watching the life of Gus and me march by, each person representing a share of it. As the surviving witness, I wanted to give the history represented in the roomful of shimmying humans busy flapping Gus kerchiefs its due. From my seat on the Igloo, I looked at the decades of loved ones, hips switching to the Stompers. I'd known some even longer than Gus—my dear first cousins Alice and Jarman were on hand—while others were friends of Gus's since his Marigny move, including the regulars of Big Daddy's Bar around the corner, all pressed and respectful. The dear and the stranger. We're all both categories to each other pretty much every day, of course.

As the Stompers packed to leave, my son-in-law Scott thanked them. "Your music meant a lot."

"We saw." The leader, Woody, nodded. "That's why we played over-time." Then the Stompers' manager pulled up outside on Dauphine to ferry them to a wedding in the Quarter that was to start in an hour. I wondered about that wedding couple, enacting a big life story chapter that day even as the hurricane approached. The world and the Stompers were about to move on.

The out-of-town guests said good-bye, antsy to leave before the storm's predicted arrival around ten o'clock. The city had set a 6 p.m. curfew, in effect until after the storm passed through. Kate and Molly thanked everyone for coming. My daughters were too young for the dignity and loss associated with their black Ann Taylor dresses and equally adult pearl ear studs. Their warmth and thanks of appreciation to everyone both broke my heart and made me proud, the signature reflex of a southern mother.

Kate and Molly had discussed Gus's ashes, deciding on the New Orleans tradition of pouring his ashes in the Mississippi on Mardi Gras morning. Families who've lost someone in the past year gather and do the honors together. Carnival was five months ahead in February.

Scott said it first: "You know, this *is* Hurricane Gus. We don't wait. We do the ashes today."

Eight of us and Kate's chocolate lab, Wilson, walked to the river. The public overlook near Gus's house had already been locked by the city as a precaution ahead of the storm. The next spot with river access was nine blocks farther in the French Quarter. We walked. When we arrived, we saw that the city had also secured the river along the Quarter, blocking off the Mississippi bank with a blocks-long length of temporary chain-link fence. I huffed.

How damn hard should it be to give Gus a ceremony? First the church service canceled by the priest and now a city barricade to ruin the ash moment too. I wasn't so daft from shock that I didn't notice that Gus was turning out to be as extraordinarily complicated to commemorate as he'd been to be married to. But just then we spotted it: a two-foot gap in the temporary Quarter fence. You could crawl through if creeping through mud in spiffy funeral clothes didn't bother you. One by one we wedged through, managing the ashes and Wilson too. Squeezing done, we stood, knocked the bonus dirt off all our black clothing, and caught our breath. We saw the gray Mississippi spread out for the thirteen-block stretch of the Quarter—we were alone. The river was empty of barges due to the storm warnings. The starter wind of Hurricane Gus rolled and ripped around us in the otherwise desolate, wide pewter sky above.

Kate and Molly picked their way down the rocky slope to the steel wool–colored water. The river and Quarter were silent, eerily soothing, it felt to me, after the day's bumps. Little splashes lapped the gray boulders at the bank. We found footholds in the rocks. Wilson chose a flat expanse of a tilted stone, too, and sat down his achy, rheumatic haunches thoughtfully. Time to start. We opened the Office Depot service bulletins.

Jack and Scott started the Book of Common Prayer lines from the liturgy: "I am the Resurrection and the Life."

With the river at their feet and the overcast sky above, Kate and Molly faced each other, both gripping a side of the rectangular black metal box. Gus's ashes were sealed inside in a plastic bag from the crematorium. The weight of his cinders had been a surprise to all of us. On reading about it, it turns out that postcremation, ashes amount to 3.5 percent of a person's body weight. For a two-hundred-pound man like Gus, the remains total around seven pounds. Kate and Molly opened the plastic bag and bent down. Gravity had its way. The cinders slipped out and caught the dark current.

The ashes bloomed in the Mississippi as we watched. "You live in Me, and you die in Me," Scott and Jack continued to recite.

It was a Bible verse I could buy because, to me, it's talking about life and love in the collective. We're inescapably in each other. We flow, blooming and swirling, all in the stream of the river's route. The moment over, I noticed that in its outrageous and off-script way, the funeral had been a fit. I'd take it. Of course I had no choice but to take it. What had been and what was.

Part 4

Taking a Step

Chapter 15

Volunteering (4)

I COLLECTED QUARTERS FROM GRANDMOTHERS FOR THE MARCH
of Dimes, and I failed at conversation with homeless men at Helping
Hand. I hope I didn't do any harm volunteering in either gig. My
own sense of possibility flexed through both, anyway. As for Meals
on Wheels, it could have taught me that time and change eventually
retool every life, Mr. Hayes's, Mrs. Shipp's, Tayleanor's, Gus's, and
mine included. Not that I connected the dots in my direction. Does
anyone do so until they must?

I have the oversized volunteer resume of lots of midlife, middle-
class Mississippi women. Among other things, I've sounded out con-
sonants with new adult readers, stuffed Mississippi Opera envelopes,
and coached spoken-word poetry in a girls' writing club. I've been a
room mother, Junior Girl Scout leader, and Sunday school teacher.
Junior League is a life stage of its own. In nine League years, I did
everything from sell cups of Sprite at the Mistletoe Marketplace
fundraiser to budget and monitor a quarter million dollars' worth
of League projects. I did hands-on cooking lessons with five-year-
olds at a West Capitol Street preschool and had entry to the city's
emergency shelter for abused children at a confidential address. It's
syrupy as well as unsurprising to say so, but I learned more than I
contributed. It's true, though.

After all the years of being one group's or another's foot soldier,
I've launched a project myself. The Academy Stories/Admissions is
an undertaking that strikes me as overdue and packs personal heat.
The project started when national audiences reacted to 2018 news
stories on legacy all-white academies still in operation in the South.

For me, though, the surprise was that people were surprised. Academies and those of us educated in them after school integration see them as town fixtures nearly as common as the municipal water tower.

Four thousand academies popped up in the South in the sixties and seventies for white children to flee public school integration. Most eventually shut down, but the survivors continue to operate, now educating a third generation of their community. Over the years, the academies have pulled so much energy out of public schools in some communities that it's common for public school teachers to send their own children to the local academy instead of where they teach. Most academies—tartly nicknamed segregation academies by opponents back in the seventies—now have slivers of minority enrollment yet remain overwhelmingly white. In academy towns, public schools are often nearly all Black, reenacting pre-1954 dual school systems.

It's a fact of human growth that the thing we dodge talking about is likely the thing that needs airing the most. (See my marriage breakup in previous pages.) It's painful but clarifying to come to terms with the truth that the Old South was, in fact, an open-air crime. The same goes for the white supremacist message of the South's neo-Confederate monuments. For white southerners, it took over a century to take the defenses down and see those history chapters with open eyes. The school-integration era is a saga still unfolding.

Besides publishing firsthand accounts of underdocumented American history, the Academy Stories is a skull self-exam for alums. If our cohort normalized our breakaway white education, what about the rest of our perceptions? In a diversity-prizing world, we took shape in a throwback pocket stitched with the wordless assumption that white is better.

I wrote an essay *Are You a Seg Academy Alum, Too? Let's Talk* for the *Bitter Southerner* in June 2019. Afterward, academy alums from across the country contacted me. They'd wondered what to make of their academy years too. Most, like me, played off that part of their youth. If you want credibility as being a progressive human, seg-academy alum isn't exactly a brand enhancer you broadcast in your Facebook profile's About section.

Yet how entitled it is to pick what I allow people to know about me, nervously cherry-picking what of my past I choose to display and what I don't. The academies do that to this day, too, soft-pedaling their origin stories. None of the school histories make mention that the US Supreme Court ended further stalling of school integration in the *Alexander v. Holmes County Board of Education* ruling in 1969.

We need to tell our academy stories for two reasons. It's a facet of American history overdue for documentation. The second reason is to reflect on what such a white bubble does to the head. It likely leaves you with a white-centered Story with a capital *S*. That's behind the two-layered meaning of the Academy Stories, the project's title, brainchild of our website designer Talamieka Brice.

Mississippi Humanities Council awarded an eighteen-hundred-dollar grant to fund launching the Academy Stories website. The grant didn't cover paying me, which chapped, but after years working for free as an easy-target woman volunteer as I have, why stop now?

The Academy Stories' online launch in October 2019 initially featured six accounts of academy alums reckoning with their schooling. For the brag: The site debut packed a cast of contributors to make *Harper's Magazine* jealous. There was novelist Steve Yarbrough, authors Alan Huffman and Kristen Green, women's studies professor Bridget Smith Pieschel, and journalist-turned-judge Lynn Watkins.

The essays are windows into the white-centered world where we swam. Boston-based novelist Steve Yarbrough's struggling family went into debt to keep him in Indianola Academy when he was in high school and away from newly integrated public classrooms. At tuition time every spring, his father stormed around the house "snarling about how [they]'d have to go without food just to keep [Steve] away from you know who."

Kristen Green's dentist grandfather cofounded Prince Edward Academy in Virginia. Their county notoriously shut down its public school system for five years in the wake of the 1954 *Brown* decision.

The closure meant Black children had no school, but white children had their new academy. Green, now in Richmond, examines her story and the community's in the praised 2015 book *Something Must Be Done About Prince Edward County*.

Writer Caroline Langston, now in the DC area, wrote about transferring to the academy in Yazoo City, Mississippi, after her father's death. She balanced gratitude for being embraced by Manchester Academy adults at a devastating time with an awareness that the school's event-filled fun wasn't for all Yazoo children. She explained, "Ninety percent of the time, daily life inside the walls of Manchester functioned as though Black people simply . . . did not exist."

The most viral essay on the site is by DC-area writer-journalist Neely Tucker. "The Nooses of Our Past" centers on returning to speak at his alma mater Starkville Academy a few years ago. As he spoke, Tucker pumped congenial but raw ferocity into the roomful of white Mississippi teenagers. Tucker encouraged them to learn about race in Mississippi, since state history revolves around it. "As mine did, your ancestors fought to preserve slavery in the Civil War," he told them. Next came "a minority-ruled terrorist regime in which white conservative Christians with serious haircuts and good jobs had fired, fined, raped, tortured and murdered political dissidents (black people) at will, and this continued until [Tucker] was child."

"Don't worry if nobody told you most of this stuff," Tucker told them. "Cuz nobody told my generation, either. All we were taught is that we were good Christians who worked hard and earned what we got. That we were the good people." Tucker was back on campus to be honored as Alumnus of the Year. I don't think he's gotten a repeat invitation since.

Courtney Clark is an alum of Strider Academy, named for Sheriff Clarence Strider who donated land for the new school in Tallahatchie County. Strider was also county sheriff at the time of Emmett Till's murder in 1955 and testified in the trial that resulted in the murderers' acquittal. Clark never heard a word at her school about the close-by lynching that stunned the world.

Once the project launched, blowback didn't take long. "These are the twisted views of an outcast, renegade, scalawag White Southerner and I assure you most White Southerners I know do not share this woman's views at all," replied one reader of a *Washington Post* story about the project. "There is nothing more pathetic than self-loathing white liberals who want to have a group pity party. Boo Freakin Hoo. My school was too white! Waaaaaaa!" wrote another.

So far thousands in Mississippi and elsewhere have been reading the pieces and talking online. People watch for new essays to drop. It's made some younger readers just now realize their academies' defiant origin—no surprise given the care the academies take to avoid their birth stories. "You know, I've heard a rumor about that, but I didn't know," an academy English teacher in her thirties told me.

Here's a disclaimer: Being a student, teacher, or parent at an academy does not make you a bad person. There. Let's breathe, white people. The book *White Fragility*—read it—points to the necessity of whites to get comfortable with being uncomfortable if we are going to learn. Some of the anxiety produced as a result of the project comes straight out of the bestseller's pages. Scrutiny comes across as an attack, producing anger or hurt. That sense of threat can stall even a willingness to reflect on academy systemics in the first place. White people have so many *feelings*.

Scholars write about white tears, the disproportionate way the emotions of white people, white women in particular, have a way of soaring to the top of a group's concern list, hijacking what's supposed to be underway. I can't say I've had any criers, true—or maybe email communication just prevents seeing them. Yet the feelings of whites—a fear of coming off looking bad or their extreme concern over the hurt feelings of other whites—overweigh mulling the big picture and the pain of others.

Early on, I got an email from possibly my favorite high school teacher, hurt that my *Bitter Southerner* essay told how I'd dressed up as a Ku Klux Klansman for Mississippi History Day in ninth grade. In the piece, I'd reported how no one blinked an eye at my DIY sheet costume as I paraded down the hall. That day I went to school thinking my outfit was funny and came home thinking the same. The teacher was wounded to read that in print. She pointed out her hard work at class preparation that year, dress-up day included. Everyone in class but me stuck to farmer overalls and pioneer bonnets. She was a dynamic, caring, hardworking teacher, I wrote back. The essay's point had been about the academy's defiant white DNA, not a burn of her or any individual for that matter. In fact, the only person I singled out in the piece was me. I was the asshole. Still, she went away from our emails hurt. We never got to the question of the academy's collective impact on our town at that pivotal moment of integration.

The South is close quarters. School allegiances produce cliquish ties, and this project circles tough history. If hypervigilance over every white person's comfort tops a full examination, truth-telling stops before it's started.

You're in a white-fragility minefield when the editor of your birthplace newspaper asks in a taped interview, "Do you feel like you're betraying your town?"

"No, I don't," I said. "I think it's healthy to have a conversation." The *Greenwood Commonwealth* editor's eventual column on the project—its title was "An Uncomfortable Topic"—was polite but disapproving. It turned out that his wife had taught at Pillow Academy for fifteen years, and their two children were graduates.

The touchiest part of bringing up the academy past for alums is that it was our parents who sent us there. You can't examine the past very long before they materialize in the line of vision. Here's what I've done: Nudge my dear parents aside. Their time was then, to be honest. This is now. That means it's my call what I do with history. I'm in charge of finding the lessons to be learned to use in the present.

That anxiety about emotional betrayal is just too much for many to overcome. One prospective contributor has been fine-tuning the wording of a promised piece for twenty-six months and counting. "I keep coming back," he said. "Those in question are very much alive."

He's a writer with two books and a play that have come out in less time. I know he's going to ultimately find his words.

"My parents only wanted the best for me." I hear that over and over. I get it. Mine did too, I've said to myself. Yet this line typically turns into a way to end the conversation rather than a springboard to think further. In my case, a comment by a fellow reporter—she is Black—rebooted my green/white ears: "When white people say, 'My parents just wanted the best for me,' don't they know that's what every parent wants? Don't they know that's what every Black parent wants too?"

Embarrassingly, I had to put my glass of sauvignon blanc down over that one. It was a throwaway comment to her over drinks but a woefully new retool for my skull. I'd always heard that line inside my white circle and nodded at face value. It's no coincidence that the words are also a squirmy general defense of therapy goers before they are ready to dig deeper into what's still at issue in their past. The words are an anxious Hail Mary to end a conversation before too many complications set in. (Please refer back to the Meals on Wheels pages on my John Lever therapy sessions and being Fine Just Fine.)

This brings us to the whataboutisms. This is the spot-on pop culture term for the type of rhetorical dirt clod thrown the project's way since before I knew there was a name for the practice. The traditional term for this logical fallacy is *tu quoque* (Latin for "you also"). It occurs when an initial claim is met with a counterclaim to dodge addressing the first point. In the Academy Stories version, the whataboutism counterclaim is me. Who am I to challenge insular white mindsets? I have one, a match with my overwhelmingly white life. I live on a nearly all-white street, jog a route of almost all-white homes and businesses, belong to a mostly white church and don't have nearly enough friends who don't look like me. I have Confederate-soldier ancestors. I have plenty of work to do, so the whataboutism lobs hit home (I can be touchily, whitely fragile, right?). I realized after a while, though, the criticism never comes from anyone heading down the woke road. It's the opposite. The criticism always comes from white people who'd rather the conversation go away. Here's my offer: if someone with better credentials would like to take over the project, it's theirs. Good luck with the no-pay part of this puppy. Until then, I'll rock on.

After a year of publishing first-person academy stories, the project widened in 2020 to public school stories as well. The new coproject is called the Admissions Project: Racism and the Possible in Southern Schools (admissionsprojects.com). Ralph Eubanks led the launch with "It Was on the Backs of Black Students" about the silent exhaustion of playing the role of the congenial model minority at his town's previously white school. Along with academy and public school stories, there's a third rail to the history too: families who packed up and opted out of the white-resistance climate. That was the case for Mississippi-born authors Paulette Boudreaux and Margaret McMullan, who wrote for the site "Put Your Hand Down, Little Colored Girl" and "She'd Segregated Me Within Her Classroom," respectively. The Boudreaux family, Black, resettled in the Bay area. The McMullans, white, resettled in the Chicago suburbs.

Stories keep coming, and, hopefully, so does the listening. A podcast production is on the schedule as well as video accounts, since plenty of potential storytellers have been allergic to essay writing since high school. The plan is also to eventually widen the conversation to explore specific ways to embrace equity and diversity in schools and in our craniums. Stories to explore: What are success stories of communities that have worked toward equity and diversity in schools? What attempts didn't pan out and why?

Despite all this talk about listening, I stopped recently halfway through a telephone call with a well-intentioned East Coast publicist. I'd wondered if a PR pro with national connections could increase the project's reach. The publicist and I met, and she generously agreed to help. Time for some open-air activism to go with people's stories, she advised. "Why don't you go to the academies and confront the principals?" she asked. "You could film it."

"I don't know," I said, which in southern-speak translates, of course, to "it'll be a cold day in hell." I'm not here to protect academy front offices, but what would a gotcha photo op accomplish except a photo? Not exactly encouraging for future conversation starters.

"Or maybe you could advocate for a bill to pass the state legislature?" she continued.

"Like what?"

"Outlaw academies! Then you'd have something to show for your work," she said.

Well, shoot. There's your answer.

I'm kidding. Outlawing private schools is not exactly a guaranteed slam dunk at the Mississippi Legislature, where its white Republican majority members quite likely send their own children and grandchildren to assorted academies across the state and have done so for three generations. Pro–public school legislators can't keep up with the maneuvers of academy-devoted legislators to hijack public funds for academies through one channel or another. In the sixties, the legislature passed a $185 tuition subsidy for every Mississippi academy student, a wink eventually stopped by the courts. Currently a provision wedged in a 2020 bill green-lights tax credits for donations to the legacy segregation academies, siphoning off $7 million in public funds to date in 2022. Another reason outlawing private schools isn't going to fly is the prime whataboutism, finger-pointing potential: Phillips Academy in Andover, Massachusetts? The Brearley School in Manhattan? Tu quoque.

"Um, I'll think about it," I told the publicist. I appreciated her time. I could tell I was a disappointment to her.

Yet she was right, in a way. Open-air activism is urgent. I think creating a place to air these suppressed stories and challenge our understanding of the past is not nothing. James Baldwin wrote that "not everything that is faced can be changed, but nothing can be changed until it is faced." Creating a space for these stories isn't everything, but it's something. Here's something else. I note in every public program that I'm not taking aim at my alma mater and the whole bleak academy history so those outside the South can nod and shout, "That's where the racists are." The Admissions Project hopefully could be a template for any cohort anywhere to examine the silos and structural inequality at work in their locale.

Meanwhile, back to the terrain here, current academy folks have a standing invitation to leave white fragility at home and take part in the project too. The approach is "Here's what I'm learning. Maybe you want to see what you think of this." In *How to Be an Antiracist*, Ibram X. Kendi sees effective antiracism as spotting racist practices and challenging them. Then it's up to people to either stand by racist practices or choose to oppose them.

Look around and it's clear that valuing diversity and equity isn't just right. It's smart. In Mississippi, towns with the most polarized racial school scapes are also towns that are shrinking. That's due to the third rail of the story again. As with the Boudreaux and McMullan families who packed up and moved, no census counts people who decide not to live in a town because of its school chasm. Looking back on the white male academy founders across Mississippi and elsewhere, they were convinced that they had "solved" their town's problem in starting a private school for whites. It turns out that within a few generations, inserting the academy into the town's ecology amounted to a slow death sentence. If given a choice, residents move to a town that has diverse, thriving public schools.

Diversity and equitable schooling pay off on the individual level as well. The world out there is lavish and big. The white student in a silo is receiving a subpar education to prepare for being part of it. A diverse education is part of any good education.

That's my project. Change is urgent. Black people are dying from our white myopia and bad faith. Change is also a long game. I want to do my part for both.

● ● ●

Looking back on my life as a volunteer and that urge, however naïve and deluded, to take steps to help, what's with all the doors? There were the front doors on the Greenwood street where I knocked for loose change for March of Dimes. Those doors were a tiny promise of a wider world than my safe, blinkered one. Thanks to the Baptist Student Union, I pushed through the glass doors of the Helping Hand Rescue Mission every Tuesday as a friend of the homeless. It was also a handy chance—pretty much my only chance—to hang out with guys. Meals on Wheels delivery was seventeen years of friendly, frail seniors opening their doors for bags of lunch and a hello. The MOW roster was always morphing. Life does as well. Through the years, maybe doors kept showing up along the way because doors just practically do keep showing up in life.

Along with the expectation to be of help, women have a particular relationship to doors as well. Even the Junior League of Jackson's 1991 cookbook *Come On In* is organized around arty photos of local doors, from the lofty Greek key–embedded six-panel one at the governor's mansion to a yellow-frame dogtrot's peeling entry. *Come On In*'s cover centers on a screen-door handle, backlit sun shining through the metal mesh. For generations, white women had access to door handles of power and help through their protected status. Many bested their men's white supremacy and raised it, tragically. History reflects few financially secure white women bothering to use their entry to help to support those shut out. Even grasping that they had the capacity to use their access was hard to see. Add to that the South's magnolia myths and the inward version of white Protestantism. The sum of all that is that heads stayed too numb, too long. In doing nothing, you perpetuate what already exists. I have perpetuated my share, I know. In my tiny way, launching the truth-telling of the Academy Stories/Admissions is my chance to at least try at doing better.

"Purpose is beyond the end you figured," noted T. S. Eliot, who, for the record, was the boy Tom Eliot a little to the north on the Mississippi River in St. Louis as a child. Deeper into "Little Gidding," part of the *Four Quartets*, he comes to those famous lines: "And the end of all our exploring / Will be to arrive where we started / And know the place for the first time." I keep seeing new layers inside my old stories and inside the old stories in the world around me. We're packages. So are our intentions. The past, the present, the hopes, the dodges, the love, and the lies. Help received, withheld, bungled, or even, most wonderfully, delivered weaves into the days and the switch points. The invitation always dangles to persist exploring where we are and how we arrived. Time and our feet are moving forward. To watch our step as we go is not nothing. Let's try.

Acknowledgments

I'm grateful to University Press of Mississippi director Craig Gill and the UPM team for putting their many and magnificent skills toward bringing this book baby to life.

I also give thanks to the Dusti Bongé Art Foundation (www .dustibonge.org), Paul Bongé, the Foundation's Board, and Director Ligia M. Römer for the use of Bongé's 1943 self-portrait *The Balcony* as the book's cover art. Biloxi-native Bongé was a recognized painter of the abstract expressionist school who, from 1956 until 1975, had regular one-woman shows at the Betty Parsons Gallery, also New York–gallery home to Jackson Pollock. As with other artists who happened to be women, of color or LGBT, the importance and memory of her work are having a new, overdue appreciation. Thanks also goes to the Mississippi Museum of Art, where *The Balcony* is part of the permanent collection.

In gestational terms, so many have cared for the project and for me during the course of the book's development. I'm grateful to my incredible Bennington Writing Seminars teachers: Susan Cheever, Phillip Lopate, Bernard Cooper, and Tom Bissell.

Thank you to the kind and brilliant editors of *Mississippi Magazine*, *Oxford American*, the *New York Times*, the *Bitter Southerner*, and *Dorothy Parker's Ashes*, who said yes to publishing and polishing early versions of parts of the book.

For the book's "Volunteering" chapters, I thank those who lived the assorted experiences along with me and let me compare my memories to theirs: Tanya Carr, Wanda Clark, Ann Kyzar, Janie Tucker, Lane Tucker, Frank and Carol Spencer, Milton Kliesch, Foster Welburn, Berry Dumas, Mable Sanders, Frances Jean Neely, Jay and Mary Ann Fontaine, Robert Wise, and all the essayists and supporters of the Admissions Project, including Stuart Rockoff and Carol Anderson of the Mississippi Humanities Council and Jane Alexander of the Community Foundation for Mississippi.

Chelsea Hodson, Teresa Nicholas, Gerry Helferich, Paulette Boudreaux, and Lauren Rhoades have been essential manuscript readers and advisers. Their reads and astute suggestions sharpened and shaped the book on its way. With time a writer's currency, I profoundly appreciate the writers who agreed to give of their own time to read *The Steps We Take* and respond with generous blurbs. Thank you again, Lauren Rhoades and Paulette Boudreaux, as well as Katy Simpson Smith, Phillip Lopate, and Lili Anolik. My cousin Alice Word has witnessed and rooted throughout the process as have the students and faculty of the Mississippi University for Women low-residency MFA program in creative writing.

I thank my late parents, who, from my earliest memories, showed me that books were a means of transport. I'd never have dreamed of being a writer if they hadn't sold me on the magic of a story from the very start. And thanks to the late Gus for the love, bounteous good and essential times shared, and, of course, to the two most wondrous daughters in the world, Kate and Molly, and to Molly's dear husband, Jack.

This book would not be what it is without those I got to meet through my purported volunteer work. You did me more good than I particularly did you, of course. I hope, at least, I did you no harm.

Last, thanks to my other half, Myron Sheen, who along with loving and journeying with me for the last twelve years, has witnessed and pulled for this book's path to print. I cheer and treasure our joint trek, the steps we take together.

Notes

Introduction

3   "Whatsoever thy hand": Eccles. 9:10 (King James Version).

6   "If you go to thinking": Jung, *The Red Book*, 253.

Chapter 1. Volunteering (1)

10–11   "You know it was the money": Everly, "Everly Brothers International Archive."

13   "They have no experience of the world": Ruefle, *Madness, Rack, and Honey*, 179–80.

15   "The Orettos" and "They gave their baby": "Greenwood Pioneers Sleep in Spot Sacred to Memory," *Greenwood Commonwealth*, November 26, 1936.

Chapter 2. In Which I'll Always Have Paris

24   "Je suis costaud": Kaplan, *French Lessons*, 89–90.

27   In truth, Doisneau's photo: Molly Driscoll, "Robert Doisneau: The Story Behind His Famous 'Kiss,'" *Christian Science Monitor*, April 14, 2012, https://www.cs monitor.com/Technology/Horizons/2012/0414/Robert-Doisneau-The-story -behind-his-famous-Kiss.

Chapter 4. A Crack in the Floor

38   iconic Imperial Hotel: Tenner, "Tokyo's Imperial Hotel Survived."

38   Fountainhead: Linda Sanders, "Fountainhead: A House At Home with Itself," *Jackson Clarion-Ledger*, January 24, 1983; and Robert Parker Adams (architect and current owner of Fountainhead), interview by author, September 11, 2022.

Chapter 8. Daffodils

57   "the richest land": Williams, *Cat on a Hot Tin Roof*, 88.

Chapter 9. Volunteering (2)

65–66   "Amazing grace!" and "When we've been": Newton and Anonymous, "Amazing Grace," 330.

67   "Jesus knows our ev'ry weakness": Scriven, "What a Friend," 163.

74   The MC president from my era: "MC Alumni Reflect on Nobles' Contributions to the School," *Jackson Clarion-Ledger*, May 27, 2007; and Jerry Mitchell, "Tabloid TV Show to Air Interview with Nobles," *Jackson Clarion-Ledger*, October 27, 1994.

75   the mission's 1961 founding: "Helping Hand to Observe Anniversary," *Jackson Clarion-Ledger*, September 23, 1961.

75   Helping Hand was adding a wing for women: Gerald Smith Jr., "Helping Hand Rescue Mission Counsels Many," *Jackson Clarion-Ledger*, December 26, 1985.

Chapter 10. Private Household Occupations

76   "irrefutable collective verity": Said, *Orientalism*, 236.

81   "service pan": Tucker, *Telling Memories*, 145.

81   "This could lead to changes": "US Will Move on Discrimination," *Jackson Clarion-Ledger*, July 2, 1965.

81   "WHITE assistant manager," "WHITE waitress," and "COLORED cook": Classifieds, *Jackson Clarion-Ledger*, July 2, 1965.

81–82 Bill Minor covered the multiday hearing: Bill Minor, interview by author at Minor's home, Jackson, Mississippi, March 17, 2014.

82   "Moderation had reared its head" and "implied purpose": Roy Reed, "TV Widens Crack in a Racial Wall; Jackson Station Has Brought Rights Hearings into Home," *New York Times*, February 21, 1965.

82   Minor remembered: Minor, interview by author, March 17, 2014.

82   fall from power of Hilly Holbrook: Stockett, *The Help*, 393.

82   publication of a tell-all book: Stockett, *The Help*, 422.

83–84 "It just pictured all white women" and "I treated them": Grace Sweet, interview by author at Sweet's home, Jackson, Mississippi, November 20, 2012.

84   The Association of Black Women Historians: Jones, *An Open Statement*.

85   "a real Fourth of July picnic": Stockett, *The Help*, 128.

85   "When I began listening" and "This is why fiction": Walker, *Alice Walker's Garden* (blog), quoted in Ashley Chaffin, "Stockett's 'The Help' Creates Tension after Successful Book and Movie Release," *Crimson White* (Tuscaloosa, AL), September 14, 2011, https://thecrimsonwhite.com/7494/culture/stocketts-the-help-creates-tension-after-successful-book-and-movie-release/.

86   "Nurse, guide, judge": de Beauvoir, *The Second Sex*, 186.

87   standpoint theory: Griffin, "Standpoint Theory," 441–53.

88   "What can we do" and "Look around?": Douglas, *Can't Quit You, Baby*, 256.

88   "post-menopausal zest": "Meaty Meadisms about America," 147.

89   In Jackson, now with an 82.8 percent: "QuickFacts: Jackson City, Mississippi," United States Census Bureau, updated July 1, 2021, https://www.census.gov/quickfacts/fact/table/jacksoncitymississippi/BZA115220.

89   "Private Household Occupations": "National Compensation Survey—Wages," US Bureau of Labor Statistics, last modified October 16, 2001, https://www.bls.gov/ocs/additional-resources/census-job-titles-see-ocsm.htm.

89   "I was always trying": Minrose Gwin, email message to author via Harper Collins senior publicity manager Gregory Henry, June 3, 2013.

92   "I thought I was at home": Douglas, *Can't Quit You, Baby*, 239.

Chapter 11. Are You a Seg Academy Alum, Too? Let's Talk

93   I'm one of the estimated 750,000: Nevin and Bills, *Schools that Fear Built*, 9.

93   2018 Senate race: Pittman, "Hyde-Smith Attended."

93   Phil Bryant: Luckett, "From Council Schools."

94   Sela Ward: Ward, *Homesick*, 54.

94   Donna Tartt: Tartt, "Team Spirit," 37–40.

94   Kathryn Stockett: "Honored Alumni," Jackson Prep, https://www.jacksonprep
      .net/alumni/honored-alumni.

94   Steve Yarbrough: Steve Yarbrough, "The Academy," *Academy Stories* (blog),
      Admissions Project: Racism and the Possible for Southern Schools, October 21,
      2020, https://admissionsprojects.com/2020/10/21/the-academy/.

94   Shepard Smith: "Donald-Smith," *Jackson Clarion-Ledger*, August 16, 1987, 6E.

94   Neely Tucker: Neely Tucker, "The Nooses of Our Past," *Academy Stories* (blog),
      Admissions Project: Racism and the Possible for Southern Schools, January 22,
      2020, https://admissionsprojects.com/2020/01/22/the-nooses-of-our-past/.

94   Britney Spears: Daly, "Britney Spears."

94   Jamie Lynn Spears: Leslie Snadowsky, "'Love 101' for Jamie," *New York Post*,
      December 23, 2007, https://nypost.com/2007/12/23/love-101-for-jamie/.

94   an estimated 43,278: Anderson, *The South*, 71.

94   The number ballooned to 236: Bolton, "The Last Stand."

95   Hyde-Smith's and Bryant's records: Jurado, "'1000 Years of Darkness'"; and Pittman,
      "Hyde-Smith's 'Public Hanging.'"

96   Mary Carol Miller remembered: Adams and Adams, *Just Trying*, 210.

97   the murderers confessed for *Look*: Huie, "The Shocking Story," 46–50.

97   "Many of these new schools": Anderson, *The South*, 69.

98   As for Bryant, he invited: Michael D. Shear and Ellen Ann Fentress, "Trump,
      Rejecting Calls to Stay Away, Speaks at Civil Rights Museum," *New York Times*,
      December 9, 2017, https://www.nytimes.com/2017/12/09/us/politics/trump-miss
      issippi-civil-rights-museum.html.

99   On National Signing Day: Nick Suss, "Signing Day: Top Recruit Jerrion Ealy Signs
      with Ole Miss," *Jackson Clarion-Ledger*, February 6, 2019, https://www.clarion
      ledger.com/story/sports/college/ole-miss/2019/02/06/national-signing-day-5-star
      -running-back-jerrion-ealy-signs/2777773002/.

99   "can provide a glimpse": Angie Thomas, email message to author, May 20, 2019.

99   "throughout the South": "'A Wonderful Education': School Blossomed from Humble
      Beginnings," *Greenwood Commonwealth*, October 20, 2016.

100   "uptown Klan": Silver, *Mississippi*, 36.

100   Patterson's 2017 obituary: "Robert Boyd 'Tut' Patterson Sr.," *Greenwood
      Commonwealth*, September 22, 2017.

100   Sylvester Hoover: Sylvester Hoover, interview by author, Greenwood, Mississippi,
      March 31, 2019.

Chapter 12. Volunteering (3)

107   "being easy in your harness": "Poet Frost, 80, Finds World Is 'Too Hurried,'"
      Baltimore Sun, March 26, 1954.
133   "You believe in God": John 14:1–3 (New International Version).
137   "Be anything you like": Merton, "Learning to Live," 11.

Chapter 13. Safely above the New Orleans Parade

148   "If a writer has to rob": Stein, "William Faulkner," 28.

Chapter 14. The Weight of Cinders

153   "And nothing is as confusing": Boully, "The *Future Imagined*," 7.

Chapter 15. Volunteering (4)

165   "snarling about": Steve Yarbrough, "The Academy," *Academy Stories* (blog),
      Admissions Project: Racism and the Possible for Southern Schools, October 21,
      2020, https://admissionsprojects.com/2020/10/21/the-academy/.
166   "Ninety percent of the time": Caroline Langston, "It's Just Like the Good Old Days
      Again," *Academy Stories* (blog), Admissions Project: Racism and the Possible for
      Southern Schools, April 8, 2020, https://admissionsprojects.com/2020/04/08/
      its-just-like-the-good-old-days-again/.
166   "As mine did": Neely Tucker, "The Nooses of Our Past," *Academy Stories* (blog),
      Admissions Project: Racism and the Possible for Southern Schools, January 22,
      2020, https://admissionsprojects.com/2020/01/22/the-nooses-of-our-past/.
171   "not everything that is faced": James Baldwin, "As Much Truth as One Can Bear,"
      New York Times, January 14, 1962.
173   "Purpose is beyond" and "And the end": Eliot, *Four Quartets*, 35, 59.

Bibliography

Adams, Natalie G., and James H. Adams. *Just Trying to Have School*. Jackson: University Press of Mississippi, 2018.

Anderson, Robert E., ed. *The South and Her Children: School Desegregation 1970-1971*. Southern Regional Council, March 1971.

Bolton, Charles C. "The Last Stand of Massive Resistance: Mississippi Public School Integration, 1970." *Mississippi History Now*, February 2009. https://mshistorynow .mdah.ms.gov/issue/the-last-stand-of-massive-resistance-1970.

Boully, Jenny. "The *Future Imagined*, the *Past Imagined*." In *Betwixt-and-Between: Essays on the Writing Life*. Minneapolis, MN: Coffee House Press, 2018.

Daly, Steven. "Britney Spears: Inside the Mind (and Bedroom) of America's Teen Queen." *Rolling Stone*, April 15, 1999. https://www.rollingstone.com/music/music-news/ britney-spears-inside-the-mind-and-bedroom-of-americas-teen-queen-188483/3/.

de Beauvoir, Simone. *The Second Sex*. Translated and edited by H. M. Parsley. New York: Vintage Books, 1989.

DiAngelo, Robin. *White Fragility: Why It's So Hard for White People to Talk About Racism*. Boston: Beacon Press, 2018.

Douglas, Ellen. *Can't Quit You, Baby*. New York: Penguin Books, 1989.

Eliot, T. S. *Four Quartets*. Orlando, FL: Harcourt, 1943.

Everly, Don. "Everly Brothers International Archive: March of Dimes (1959)." Everly Brothers International. YouTube video, 0:38. https://www.youtube.com/watch?v=rEmAG9Jfgro.

Griffin, Em. "Standpoint Theory of Sandra Harding and Julia T. Wood." In *A First Look at Communication Theory*, 441–53. New York: McGraw-Hill Education, 2009.

Gwin, Minrose. *The Queen of Palmyra*. New York: Harper Perennial, 2010.

Horney, Karen. *Feminine Psychology*. New York: W. W. Norton, 1993.

Huie, William Bradford. "The Shocking Story of Approved Killing in Mississippi." *Look*, January 24, 1956.

Jones, Ida E., Daina Ramey Berry, Tiffany M. Gill, Kali Nicole Gross, and Janice Sumler-Edmond. *An Open Statement to the Fans of The Help*. Association of Black Women Historians, August 12, 2011. https://abwh.org/2011/08/12/an-open-statement-to-the-fans -of-the-help/.

Jung, C. G. *The Red Book*. Edited by Sonu Shamdasani. New York: W. W. Norton, 2009.

Jurado, Joe. "'1000 Years of Darkness' Will Begin If Mississippi Elects Its First Black Senator, According to Its Governor." *Root*, January 8, 2020. https://www.theroot.com/ 1000-years-of-darkness-will-begin-if-mississippi-elects-1840885059.

Kalich, Tim. "An Uncomfortable Topic." *Greenwood Commonwealth*, January 30, 2021.

Kaplan, Alice. *French Lessons*. Chicago: University of Chicago Press, 1993.

Kendi, Ibram X. *How to Be an Antiracist*. New York: One World, 2019.

Luckett, Robert. "From Council Schools to Today's Fight for Public Ed." *Jackson Free Press*, February 15, 2017. https://www.jacksonfreepress.com/news/2017/feb/15/council-schools-todays-fight-public-ed/.

"Meaty Meadisms about America." *Life*, September 14, 1959.

Merton, Thomas. "Learning to Live." In *Love and Living*, edited by Naomi Burton Stone and Brother Patrick Hart. Orlando, FL: Harcourt, 1965.

Nevin, David, and Robert E. Bills. *The Schools that Fear Built.* Washington, DC: Acropolis Books, 1976.

Newton, John, and Anonymous. "Amazing Grace." In *Baptist Hymnal*, 330. Nashville: Convention Press, 1991.

Paris, Bernard J. *Karen Horney: A Psychoanalyst's Search for Self-Understanding.* New Haven, CT: Yale University Press, 1994.

Pittman, Ashton. "Hyde-Smith Attended All-White 'Seg Academy" to Avoid Integration." *Jackson Free Press*, November 23, 2018. https://www.jacksonfreepress.com/news/2018/nov/23/hyde-smith-attended-all-white-seg-academy-avoid-in/.

Pittman, Ashton. "Hyde-Smith's 'Public Hanging' Quip Bombs in State with Most Lynchings." *Jackson Free Press*, November 11, 2018. https://www.jacksonfreepress.com/news/2018/nov/11/hyde-smiths-public-hanging-quip-bombs-state-most-l/.

Rhodes, CJ. "Opinion: Why the History of Lynching Is No Laughing Matter." *Jackson Free Press*, November 14, 2018. https://www.jacksonfreepress.com/news/2018/nov/14/opinion-why-history-lynching-no-laughing-matter/.

Ruefle, Mary. Madness, Rack, and Honey: Collected Lectures. Seattle: Wave Books, 2012.

Said, Edward W. *Orientalism.* New York: Penguin Books, 2003.

Scriven, Joseph. "What a Friend We Have in Jesus." In *Baptist Hymnal*, 163. Nashville: Convention Press, 1991.

Silver, James W. *Mississippi: The Closed Society.* New York: Harcourt, Brace, and World, 1966.

Stein, Jean. "William Faulkner: The Art of Fiction No. 12." *Paris Review* 12 (Spring 1956).

Stockett, Kathryn. *The Help.* New York: G. P. Putnam's, 2009.

Sweet, Grace, and Benjamin Bradley. *Church Street: The Sugar Hill of Jackson, Mississippi.* Charleston, SC: History Press, 2013.

Tartt, Donna. "Team Spirit." *Harper's Magazine*, April 1994.

Tenner, Edward. "How Tokyo's Imperial Hotel Survived a 1923 Earthquake." *Atlantic*, April 1, 2011. https://www.theatlantic.com/technology/archive/2011/04/how-tokyos-imperial-hotel-survived-a-1923-earthquake/73306/.

Thomas, Angie. *The Hate U Give.* New York: Balzer and Bray, 2017.

Trethewey, Natasha. "Domestic Work, 1937." In *Domestic Work.* Saint Paul, MN: Graywolf Press, 2000.

Tucker, Susan. *Telling Memories among Southern Women.* Baton Rouge: Louisiana State University Press, 1988.

Walker, Alice. *The Color Purple.* New York: Harcourt Brace Jovanovich, 1982.

Ward, Sela. *Homesick.* New York: HarperCollins, 2002.

Williams, Tennessee. *Cat on a Hot Tin Roof.* New York: New Directions Books, 1975.

Credits

Earlier versions of Chapter 3, "Renovation," and Chapter 8, "Daffodils," originally appeared in *Mississippi Magazine*, September/October 1999 and March/April 1999.

Chapter 4, "A Crack in the Floor," originally appeared in *Dorothy Parker's Ashes*, October 16, 2022.

Chapter 5, "The Rubble of My Marriage, Hidden by Katrina's," Chapter 7, "The Divorcée's French Class," and Chapter 13, "Safely above the New Orleans Parade" originally appeared in the *New York Times*, August 2007, October 2014, and September 2011.

Earlier versions of Chapter 6, "Lessons in the Past Tense," and Chapter 10, "Private Household Occupations," originally appeared in the *Oxford American*, August 2011 and July 2014.

An earlier version of Chapter 11, "Are You a Seg Academy Alum, Too? Let's Talk," originally appeared in *The Bitter Southerner*, June 6, 2019.

About the Author

Photo courtesy of the author

A lifelong Mississippian born in the Delta, Ellen Ann Fentress turns her reporter's eye to the deep meaning and messages of her Deep South life and the culture surrounding her.

Her work, sometimes wry, sometimes tragic, often centers on the question of reckoning with the pathology of whiteness both in the individual life and in the collective systems around us. Fentress brings to bear reflections on Mississippi as both the painful historic epicenter of American injustice and the home to an equal legacy of resistance and triumph.

Four years ago, she launched The Admissions Project: Racism and the Possible in Southern Schools, an online platform for first-person accounts from the post-integration South (www.admissionsprojects .com.). The stories include accounts from graduates of the overnight all-white "segregation academies," many still in operation, as well as from public schools.

Her 2016 documentary *Eyes on Mississippi*, a fifty-six-minute film on the midcentury reporting of iconic civil rights journalist W. F. "Bill" Minor, has screened at universities and cultural venues across the country.

A contributor to the *New York Times, Washington Post, The Atlantic*, and *Oxford American*, among other publications, she teaches in the Mississippi University for Women's creative writing MFA program. Her website: www.ellenannfentress.com.

An MFA from Bennington College, she has received literary fellowships and awards from the Mississippi Arts Commission, Greater Jackson Arts Council, the Southern Women Writers Conference, and the William Faulkner-William Wisdom Creative Writing Competition.